TEXAS FESTIVALS

Texas Festivals

The most complete guide to celebrations in the Lone Star State

by Dawn Albright

Printed in the United States of America

Publisher's Cataloging in Publication
(Prepared by Quality Books Inc.)
Albright, Dawn, 1963-
Texas festivals : the most complete guide to celebrations in the Lone Star State / Dawn Albright. --
p. cm.
ISBN 0-9628824-1-0
1. Texas--Description and travel--1981- --Guide-books. 2. Festivals--Texas. I. Title.

F384.3 917.64
QB191-207

Library of Congress Catalog Card Number: 91-60652

Cover design and illustration by Harrington Designs, Austin

Cover photo of Charro Days Fiesta, Brownsville, courtesy Texas Department of Commerce

Palmetto Press
619 Betty Street
El Campo, Texas 77437

To Richard and Nathan

ACKNOWLEDGEMENTS

I had fun writing this book, going to festivals and meeting interesting people. Of course, I had to work hard to finish it, spending hours in the car, on the phone, in front of a computer screen and in the library. Many people helped me overcome obstacles and move forward.

The staff of the El Campo Library was endlessly helpful, friendly and supportive. Thank you, Frances Arrambide, Laverne Bacak, Annete Balcar, Lori Kocurek and Rose Pasak.

Special thanks, for a multitude of favors, go to Chris Barbee, Sherry Roddy and all the great people at the *El Campo Leader-News.*

I couldn't have accomplished a thing without someone to take care of my son, so I thank Rosemary Alejo, Belinda Garcia and the folks at Oakwood Day School.

Others who helped out in various ways include Theresa Earle of Creative Publishing, Supriya Nayalkar, Amy Albright, Lane Goldsmith, Laura Jo and Doug Tabony, and Martha and Paulo Pinto.

I thank my husband, Richard Goldsmith, for his encouragement and 24-hour advice service. And my mother, Dianne Albright, for teaching me to read and write, and father, Duffey Albright, for teaching me to persevere.

Of course, I must thank all the chamber of commerce and festival committee people who provided me with most of the information in this book. For photographs, I thank Mari Schnell of the Texas Tourism Division and the many newspapers who contributed prints from their files.

And sincere appreciation goes out to all the dedicated volunteers who make festivals happen.

CONTENTS

★

How This Book Works

This book is arranged so that whenever you have a free weekend, you can plan an affordable outing with friends or family. The state is divided into three arbitrary sections: North and Northeast Texas, South and Southeast Texas, and West Texas and the Panhandle. Within each region, festivals are grouped according to the month in which they happen. Within each month, they are arranged chronologically, for the most part.

In each festival listing, you'll find an address and phone number to contact for more information on parking, accommodations, and event schedules. Most listings include an approximate admission price. If there's no admission noted, that means the information was unavailable.

Say you live in Dallas, it's August, and your sister-in-law and her kids are visiting from Iowa. You've taken them shopping, to the zoo, dozens of night spots, Shakespeare in the Park, White Rock Lake, the Museum of Fine Arts, the Texas School Book Depository, and John Neely Bryan's cabin.

Now they want to see rural Texas, and you're ready to get out of that hot town. So you open up your trusty copy of *Texas Festivals*, look in the North and Northeast section of the book, under August, find an event that looks fun, then call them. You can head up to Paris, across rolling, wooded terrain for the Northeast Texas Heritage Festival. Or, you can take a shorter trip to Denton for the North Texas State Fair. Your relatives will see some beautiful Texas countryside and get a taste of real Texas culture.

If you're interested in a particular town, look it up in the index. Or, if know the name of a great festival, but don't remember where it is, you can look in the index for that.

It's important to confirm festival activities before you take that hour or two drive. Most of these shabangs are put on by volunteers, and volunteers get burned out, so every once in awhile, a festival ceases to exist. Admission fees, dates and activities may also change from year to year, so call or write before you go.

Most of the phone numbers are for chambers of commerce or tourist bureaus. But many are to people's homes or offices, especially in the smaller towns, so please be nice when you call. And don't be surprised if you hear tools clanging or babies babbling in the background.

This book doesn't include every festival in Texas, by any means. It focuses on non-profit, community generated celebrations with multiple activities that attract visitors from out of town. Most of these are suitable for children.

You may want or need more information in you adventures around the state. The Texas Department of Highways and Public Transportation offers some great free info.

The Texas State Travel Guide is a 248-page book that tells a little about most of the towns and attractions in the state. It's got plenty of color photos, and lists state parks, lakes and national forests.

The Texas Calendar of Events is a small booklet, issued quarterly, listing hundreds of events all over the state from museum exhibits to community theatre performances. The highway department will also send you a free map.

Write or call:
Travel and Information Division
P.O. Box 5064
Austin, Tx. 78763
512/483-3706

Texas Highways magazine, the Highway Department's official monthly travel publication, is known as one of the best travel magazines in the nation. It's available at most newsstands or by subscription. Write to *Texas Highways*, P.O. Box 5016, Austin, Tx. 78763.

★

About Texans and their Festivals

In spite of all the stereotypes, Texans are a varied bunch. As you travel from town to town, you meet all kinds of people -- rough and timid, eccentric and simple. All live in a state that's changing, growing and diversifying.

The best way to get to know the people of Texas, their traditions and their folklore, is to attend their parties. Their celebrations and festivals. Here, you'll find out what's really important to us.

Food is of major concern, as shown by the smoke from the myriad of barbecue, bean and chili cook-offs. Festivals celebrate every kind of fruit, vegetable and grain that Texans grow or eat.

You'll find music and dancing are dear to many Texans when you go to fiddlers contests, polka festivals, conjunto concerts and street dances.

Texans love their children, as you'll learn when you see children's parades, face painting, carnivals, sack races, kiddie rodeos, and children performing dance, music, and drama.

The way we make our livings stands near the top of the priority list, of course. Many festivals celebrate industry, from agriculture to oil.

History is important to many Texans, especially after the hard times we saw during the 1980s with the collapse of the oil and real estate markets.

Although we cherish our past glories of cotton, cattle and oil, we are trying to come to terms with a new world. That's what this book is about -- the old and the new in the celebrations that mirror our culture.

As many communities watched the present crumble around them, they looked to the past for what they could save, and to find guidance and strength to face the future.

They researched their pioneer heritage, restored their old buildings, and started museums to preserve history. They recognized that times change, economies change, and Texans, for the most part, have been able to adjust. Now, many festivals celebrate the bygone days when cotton and cattle were king, or periods of oil booms in their towns. Many honor the people who settled the towns, and many showcase pre-industrial ways of doing things, known as heritage arts.

Albany's outdoor musical, the Fort Griffin Fandangle, dramatizes the settling of that area. Navasota celebrates its well-preserved Victorian archectiture. Pleasanton honors its rancing heritage with the Cowboy Homecoming. The Mineral Wells Crazy Water Festival remembers the time when that town was a health resort.

While some towns commemorate the olden days, others focus on today. Many events center around old but thriving industries like rice, peaches, seafood, watermelon, and dairy products. Others give the stage to newcomers on the Texas scene like apples and crawfish. Timber, chicken, salt, leather, onions and citrus also appear as festival stars around the state.

Texas' natural beauty inspires many people to celebrate, especially in the spring when wildflowers, dogwoods and azaleas bloom. Woodville's Dogwood Festival, Newton's Wild Azalea Spring Festival and the Highland Lakes Bluebonnet Trail all show off the state's bright colors. In the fall, Canadian's Fall Foliage Festival and Winnsboro's Autumn Trails have been drawing people for years to see the trees turn gold and red. Several towns in East Texas celebrate the forest, while those on the coast clelebrate the beauty of the sea.

Finally, our diverse ethnic mix makes for some interesting festivals. Wurstfest in New Braunfels is one of the largest celebrations of German heritage in the country. Westfest in West, another big one, focuses on Czech culture. You'll find many more German and Czech festivals. Numerous towns hold celebrations on the Mexican holidays Diez y Seis and Cinco de Mayo. Charro Days in Brownsville centers around Mexican-style rodeo, called *charreada*. Nederland celebrates its Dutch and Cajun heritage. Castroville, the only Alsatian settlement in the United States, celebrates St. Louis Day.

Several festivals focus on all or most of the ethnic groups in Texas. The largest of these, and one you shouldn't miss, is the Texas Folklife Festival at the Institute of Texan Cultures in San Antonio. Others include the General Sam Houston Folklife Festival in Huntsville and Hidalgo Borderfest.

Wherever you go in Texas, I'm sure you'll be welcomed. Go ahead, jump into the fun and make yourself at home. Participate or just watch, as long as you have a good time.

★

North and Northeast Texas

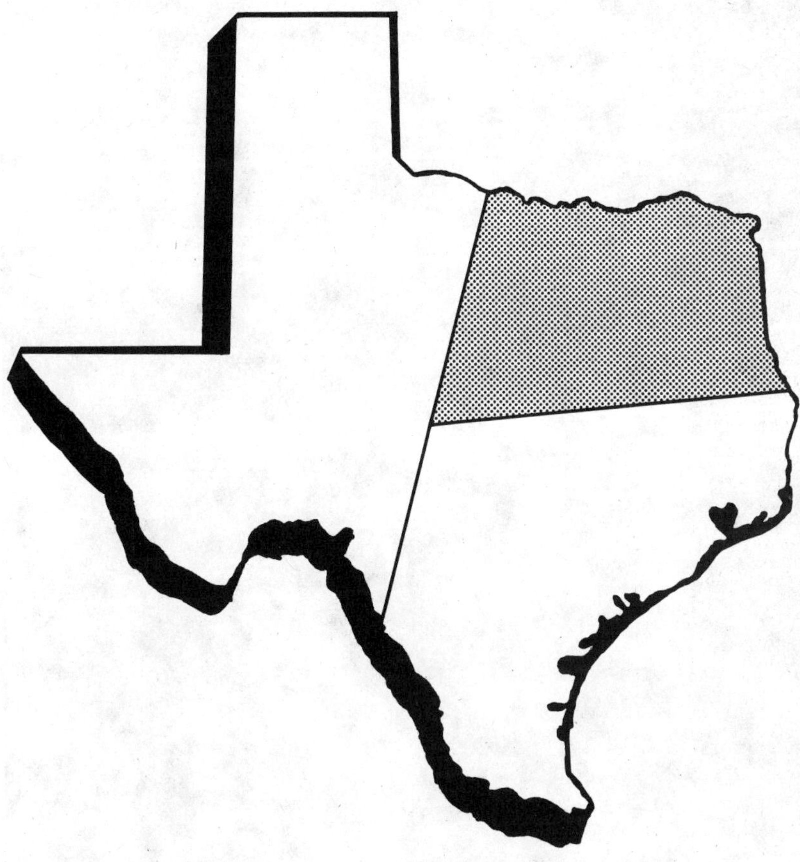

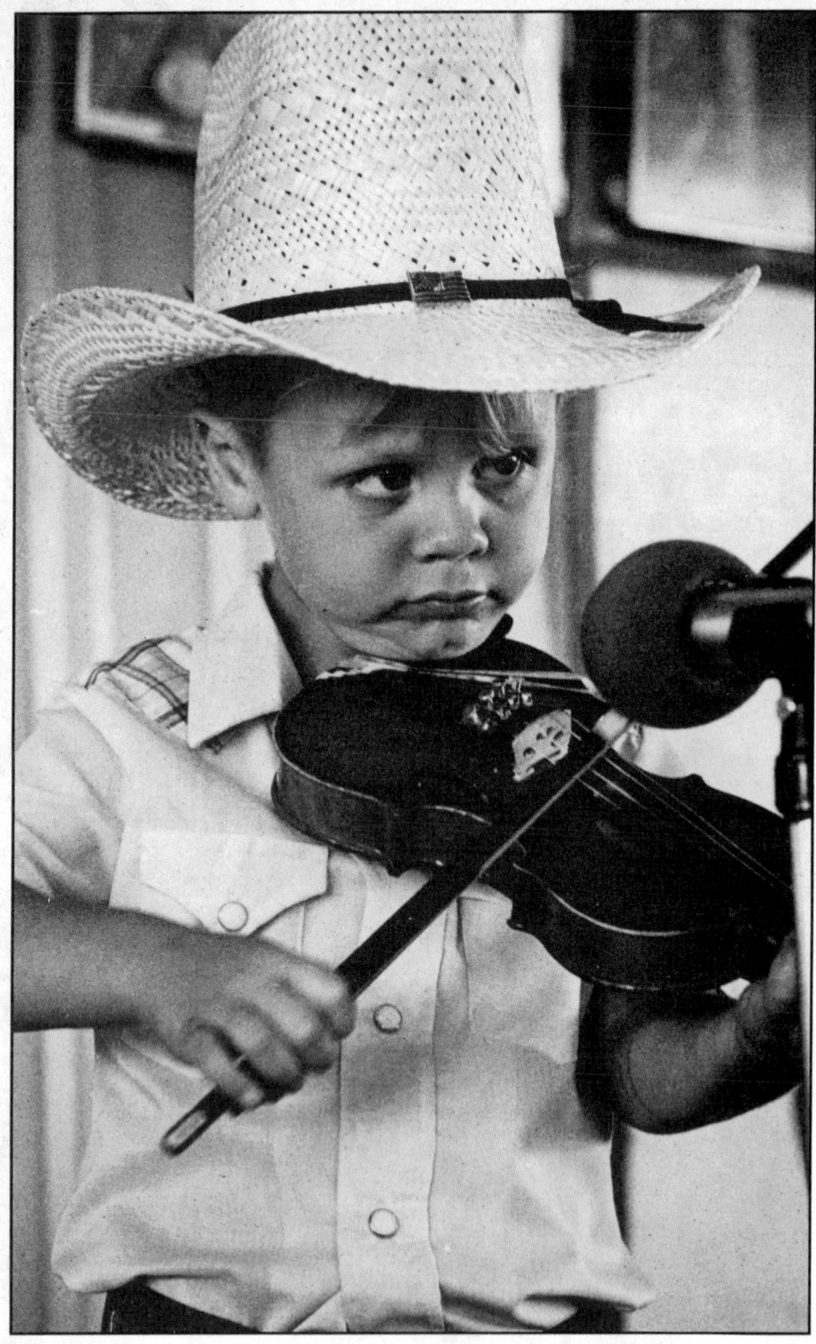

A boy plays fiddle during the Stonewall Peach JAMboree. Photo courtesy Texas Department of Commerce.

MARCH

Granbury
General Granbury's Birthday Party and Bean Cook-off
First Saturday in March
Granbury Convention and Visitors Bureau, P.O. Box 277, Granbury 76048, 817/573-5548
Admission: free

This salute to Civil War Gen. Hiram B. Granbury features a parade, bean cook-off, rib cook-off, live entertainment all day, food booths and games. Entries in the cook-off may be any variety of bean — they've even had pink beans.

Belton
Texas Polka Music Awards Festival
Second weekend in March
Texas Polka Music Association, 11511 Katy Fwy., Suite 423, Houston 77079, 713/556-9595, 713/468-2494; or Belton County Expo Center, 1-800-444-9309
Admission: $8.50

Three days of polka music and dancing attract people from all over Texas and the U.S. for this celebration of one of the state's most popular forms of ethnic music. More than 30 nationally and regionally known bands entertain at the Belton County Expo Center. Many polka musicians come from Czech ancestry, but the Polish, German, Mexican and Cajun cultures also produce fine polka music. You'll hear the accordion, saxaphone, trumpet and guitar played in the polka ensembles.

Julius Tupa, director of the Texas Polka Music Association, said the group chose Belton for the event for its central location. This organization, along with the *Texas Polka News*, works to gain respect and recognition for polka music.

Besides music and dancing, visitors will find a polka mass Sunday morning, arts and crafts, and plenty of food.

Dublin
Saint Patrick Festival
Weekend closest to St. Patrick's Day — Thursday through Sunday
Dublin Chamber of Commerce, 213 E. Blackjack, Dublin 76446, 817/445-3422
Admission: $1, includes parking

This three-day celebration features a parade, a Miss Dublin

Pageant, a dance, contests, arts and crafts, a stage show, and food booths. You'll find a variety of games, including hog calling, milk drinking, ice cream eating, hay throwing and a cow chip toss.

Dublin is home to the Aurora Dairy, said to be the largest in the world.

Palestine
Texas Dogwood Trails

Last two weekends in March and first weekend in April
Texas Dogwood Trails, 400 N. Queen, Palestine 75802, 903/729-7275 or Palestine Area Chamber of Commerce, P.O. Box 1177, Palestine 75801, 903/723-3014

Palestine's Dogwood Trails celebrates the white blooms of the dogwood trees that signal spring in East Texas. The town organizes a parade, arts and crafts fair, live music performances, and a fun run.

APRIL

Winnsboro
Spring Trails
April
Winnsboro Chamber of Commerce, 201 W. Broadway, Winnsboro, 75494, 903/342-3666
Admission: free

This celebration of the forest's springtime beauty grew out of the success of Winnsboro's Autumn Trails. Events go on each weekend in April except Easter. A classic car parade, live entertainment, a trail ride, and a barn dance are some of the month's scheduled activities.

Visitors can also see an herb and nursery show at Heritage Mall, the town's restored train depot. Events are scheduled differently each year, so call ahead to see what's happening when.

Lampasas
Bluebonnet Fair
First Saturday in April
Lampasas County Chamber of Commerce, P.O. Box 627, Lampasas 76550, 512/556-5172
Admission: free

A drive through the bluebonnet-covered hills brings you to Lampasas, where the courtyard square fills up with people for a celebration of spring. Activities include a big fish fry, a bicycle and tricycle decorating contest and parade, live music all day and an arts and crafts fair.

Quitman
Dogwood Fiesta
First two weeks in April
Quitman Scenic Association, P.O. Box 790, Quitman 75783, chamber of commerce at 903/763-4411
Admission: free

A designated car route through the woods near Quitman takes visitors trough an area thick with dogwood trees. A footpath connecting with the auto trail leads walkers around a small lake and past hundreds of the white-blossomed trees.

Activities during the Dogwood Fiesta include an arts and crafts market, style show, parade, and a bass tournament.

Kilgore
Glory Days Festival
Second weekend in April, unless Easter falls on that date
Kilgore Chamber of Commerce, P.O. Box 1582, Kilgore 75662, 903/984-5022
Admission: free

This celebration hearkens back to the 1930s, when Kilgore was an oil boomtown. Activities include a parade, re-enactments of events that took place in the 1930s, a dance, fun run, fiddling contest, arts and crafts, and food booths. You'll find competitive events such as dominoes, horseshoes, egg toss and weight lifting.

Burkburnett
Boomtown Blowout/Bike Race and Fun Run
Third weekend in April, depending on Easter
Burkburnett Chamber of Commerce, 412 N. Ave. C, Burkburnett 76354, 817/569-3305
Admission: free except for dance

Burkburnett acquired the nickname Boomtown because it grew up during the oil boom in the early part of this century. About 900 cyclists come for the 100K, 32-mile, 23-mile and 7-mile races, as well as 5K and 10K runs. On Saturday visitors can enjoy a parade, live entertainment in the park, games, arts and crafts, food booths, and a dance.

Terrell
Heritage Jubilee
Mid-April
Terrell Chamber of Commerce, P.O. Box 97, Terrell 75160, 903/563-5703
Admission: free

Terrell's Heritage Jubilee includes a tour of historic homes, a prettiest baby contest, a square dance festival, and a chili cook-off. There's also live entertainment, an arts and crafts fair, food booths, an antique car show, and a carnival.

Muenster
Germanfest
Last weekend in April
Muenster Chamber of Commerce, P.O. Box 479, Muenster 76252, 817/759-2227
Admission: $4

Muenster's festival attracts folks who like to eat and folks

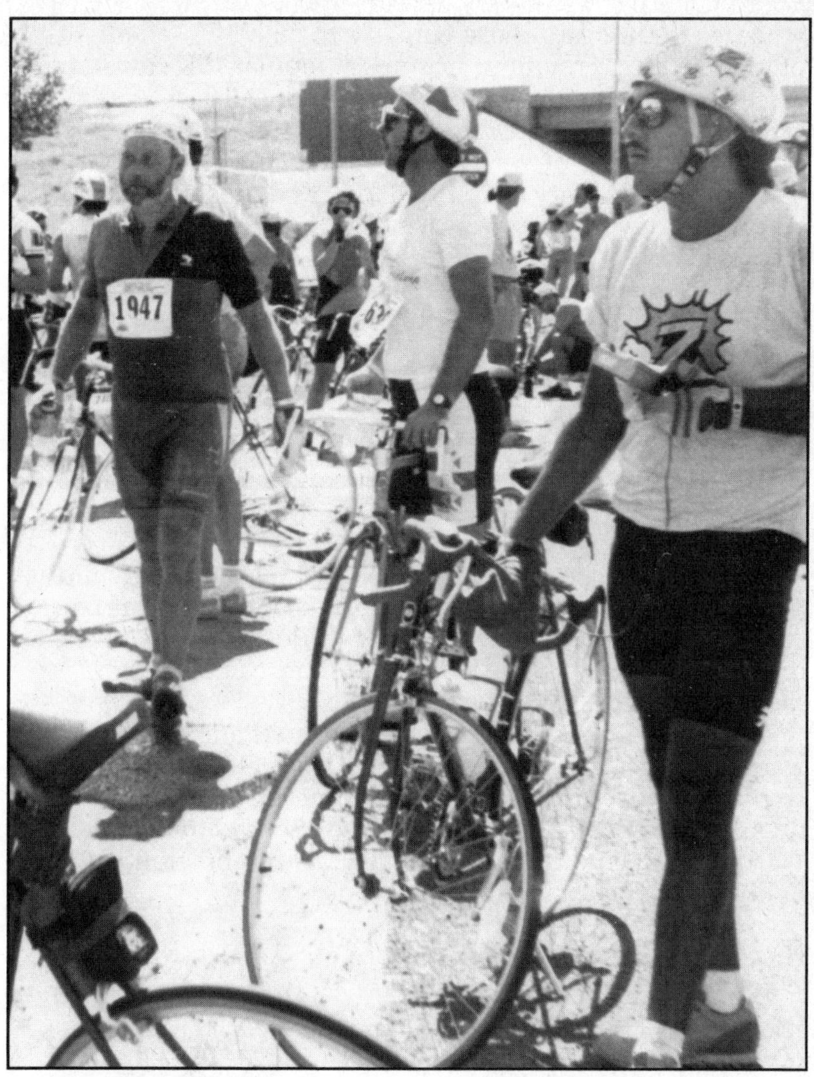

Racers take a rest during the Burkburnett Boomtown Blowout Bike Race and Fun Run. Photo courtesy *Burkburnett Informer-Star*.

who like to run. And those who like to do both —about 50,000 of them in all. Germanfest features a popular 15K run attended by several thousand people each year, as well as a 5K run, bike rally and volksmarch. Other competitive activities include arm wrestling and tug-of-war.

You'll enjoy plenty of German food and music all weekend, starting Friday afternoon and ending Sunday night. An arts and crafts fair, a carnival, and dances under the pavilion keep visitors well-entertained. There's also a brisket, sausage, and rib cook-off.

Pittsburg
Chickfest
Last Saturday of April
Camp County Chamber of Commerce, 202 Jefferson, Pittsburg 75686, 903/856-3442
Admission: free

Chickfest, as the name suggests, celebrates the main industry in the Pittsburg area – poultry. A major event is the chicken cook-off, co-sponsored by Pilgrim's Pride, with four chicken dish categories. After the judging, visitors can buy samples of the contest dishes.

The Tournament of Eggcellence includes an egg toss, a wagonload-of-eggs race and a few other messy events. For children, there's the baby chick costume contest, in which kids dress up like chicks, as well as sack races and other games.

You'll find entertainment all day, an arts and crafts fair, food booths, and a nighttime street dance.

Hughes Springs, Linden and Avinger
Wildflower Trails of Texas
Last full weekend in April
Wildflower Trails of Texas, Box 218, Hughes Springs 75656, Hughes Springs: 903/639-2351; Avinger: 903/562-1255; Linden: 903/756-3106
Admission: free

The three-town area of Hughes Springs, Linden and Avinger in Cass County hosts the first chartered wildflower trail in Texas. Each town plans various activities during the last weekend in April, when wildflower blooms are often the most profuse.

Hughes Springs has a parade, treasure hunt, art exhibit, dunking booth, street dance, home tour, teen dance, cake walk, entertainment in the park and crafts show.

Linden hosts a Little Miss Wildflower Trails Pageant, a Miss Wilted Wildflower pageant, a dance, 5K run, walk-a-thon and the Wildflower Road Race, sanctioned by the U.S. Cycling Federation. Other events include a barbecue cook-off, parade, arts and crafts fair, art gallery, street dance, carnival and old picture display.

In Avinger, there's a trail ride, a flea market, a treasure hunt, western day, a youth carnival, a parade, and a chili cook-off. A log-splitting contest, dance, and a Sunday dinner round out the events.

Waskom
Waskom Round-up
Fourth Saturday in April
Waskom Service League, P.O. Box 546, Waskom 75692, call the Travel Information Center at 903/687-2547
Admission: free

Celebrating life in East Texas, this festival features contests, arts and crafts exhibits, a stage show, food booths, and a children's art area. The T.C. Lindsey & Co. General Store in Waskom makes an interesting stop. It carries lots of old-fashioned items and has been in several Disney films.

MAY

Ennis
National Polka Festival
First weekend in May
Ennis Chamber of Commerce, P.O. Box 1177, Ennis 75119, 214/875-2625
Admission: free except for dance halls; $5 ticket gains admission to all four halls

This large Czech festival starts Saturday with a parade, followed by street entertainment including gymnastics, folk dancing and a 10K and fun run.

You'll also find regional arts and crafts for sale, plenty of Czech food, such as kolaches (pastry) and klobase (sausage). Some of the best polka bands in the state play in four halls around Ennis for polka and waltz lovers.

Howe
Founder's Day
First Saturday in May
Howe Chamber of Commerce, P.O. Box 250, Howe 75059, call *Howe Enterprise* at 903/532-6012
Admission: free

Howe Founder's Day includes a parade, bicycle rally (10K, 35K and 60K), horseshoe pitching and other contests, an arts and crafts fair, live entertainment, and food booths.

Gladewater
East Texas Gusher Days
First full weekend in May
Gladewater Chamber of Commerce, P.O. Box 1409, Gladewater 75647, 903/845-2626
Admission: free

Gusher Days, begun in 1986, looks back to the East Texas oil boom of the 1930s. Activities include a parade, chili cook-off, dance, a two-act musical comedy, arts and crafts, food booths, a carnival, and a variety of games.

Marlin
Marlin Festival Days
First weekend in May
Marlin Chamber of Commerce, P.O. Box 369, Marlin 76661, 817/883-2171

Admission: $3 adult

Marlin's oak tree-shaded city park provides a comfortable setting for arts and crafts, live entertainment, a barbecue cook-off and food booths. Other activities include a parade, 5K run, three dances with live bands and a carnival. You'll find horse-shoe, tug-of-war and bucket brigade contests.

Mineola
Mineola May Days
First weekend in May
Mineola Chamber of Commerce, P.O. Box 68, Mineola 75773, 903/569-2087
Admission: free

May Days features a parade, dance, contests, arts and crafts fair, stage show, food booths, sidewalk sale and an antique car rally.

Bonham
Bois D'Arc Festival
Third weekend in May
Bonham Chamber of Commerce, First and Center St., Bonham 75418, 903/583-4811
Admission: free

This festival, named after the Bois D' Arc (also known as horseapple) tree, began in 1986 as part of the Texas Sesquicentennial celebration. It now includes a parade, a dance, 10K and 3K runs, historical crafts and displays, games, and an arts and crafts fair. There's also live entertainment, food booths and sometimes hot air balloons.

The bois d'arc tree is also called Osage Orange, because the Osage Indians used the wood to make bows and other things. If you're familiar with French, you know bois d'arc means "wood of the bow." The tree is fairly common in Northeast Texas, and can be recognized in the late summer and fall by its large, bumpy, green "apples." Some people believe if you put horseapples in your kitchen cabinets, you won't have any cockroaches.

Gainesville
Depot Days
Third weekend in May
Gainesville Chamber of Commerce, P.O. Box 518, Gainesville 76240, 817/665-2831
Admission: free

Gainesville raises money to preserve the old Santa Fe Railroad Depot with this festival. It starts Friday night with a street dance, and continues Saturday with games, country and bluegrass music, an arts and crafts fair, a bike rally, a fun run, antique car show, and a tour of historic homes. A private museum of Coca-cola memorabilia is open to the public during Depot Days.

Gilmer
Cherokee Rose Festival and Tours
Late May
Upshur County Chamber of Commerce, P.O. Box 854, Gilmer 75644, 903/843-2413
Admission: free

This celebrates the Cherokee Indian history of the area and the Cherokee roses that bloom along an old Indian trail.

Activities include guided tours of the Cherokee Trace, a quilt show, fun run, antique and classic car show, arts and crafts, stage show, and a turtle race. Visitors can participate in oppossum calling and other contests.

Cherokee Rose is the Wild Pink Rose, *Rosa setigera*. According to legend, an Indian planted the flowers to mark the trail. The Cherokee trace, which ran all the way into Oklahoma, divided Henderson and Nacogdoches counties when they were the main counties in northeast Texas. After the Indians were gone, other people used the trail, which at one time was called the Old Military Road. Now, it's mostly a small country road, although highways run alongside it in some places. In Upshur County, part of the trace is blacktopped.

Marshall
Stagecoach Days
Third weekend in May
Marshall Chamber of Commerce, P.O. Box 520, Marshall 75671, 903/935-7868
Admission: free

Marshall celebrates its heritage as an important transportation center with this fun-filled weekend. Throughout its history, the town has been home to a major train depot, stagecoach stop and pony express station.

The festival offers stagecoach rides, lumberjack competition and the Miss Loose Caboose Contest. This farce of a beauty pageant features women dressed as forms of transportation. That's right, some dress as cars, some as canoes, making the

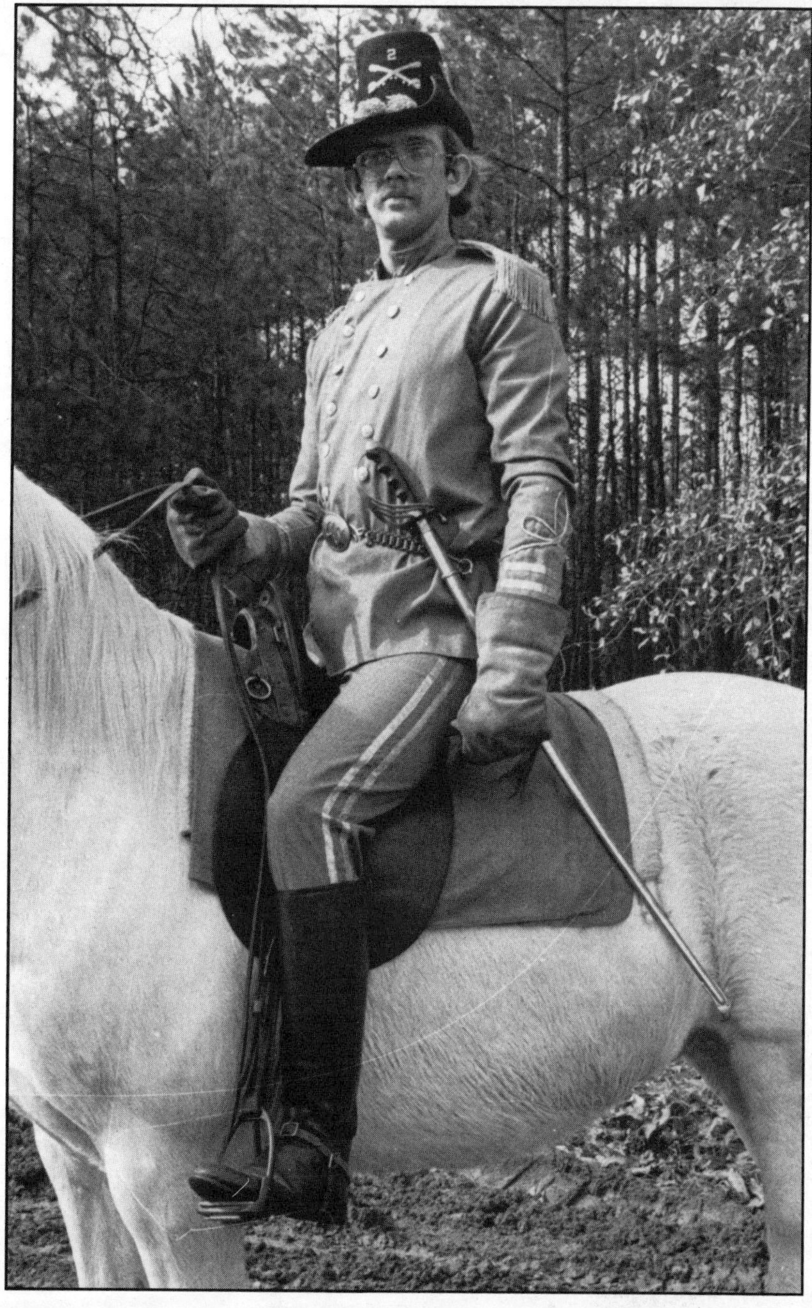

A rider wears a Confederate uniform during Marshall Stagecoach Days. Photo courtesy Texas Department of Commerce.

event hilarious. The show includes a luncheon and style show.

Other activities include a parade, street dance, historic homes tour, dinner theatre, fiddler's contest, children's games, arts and crafts, and food booths.

Rusk
Memorial Day Fair on the Square
Saturday before Memorial Day
Rusk Chamber of Commerce, P.O. Box 67, Rusk 75785, 903/683-4242
Admission: free

Held on the courthouse square, this event features a variety of games and contests, an ugly pickup truck contest, an arts and crafts fair, food booths, all-day entertainment, a cake walk, and a street dance.

While you're there, take a ride on the Texas State Railroad, an antique train in Rusk State Park that makes 25-mile trips to Palestine.

Visitors to Waxahachie's Gingerbread Trail admire the architecture of the Ellis County Courthouse. Photo courtesy Texas Department of Commerce.

JUNE

Gatesville
Shivaree
First Saturday in June
Gatesville Chamber of Commerce, 2401 S. Highway 36, Gatesville 76528, 817/865-2617
Admission: $1

Back in the olden days, when country folk got married,they usually couldn't afford a trip to Hawaii or Cozumel, so they just went home for their honeymoon. Their neighbors, with a mixture of mischief and affection, would often go to the young couple's house bearing food and drink and stand outside singing songs.

These days, the people in Gatesville aren't celebrating anyone's marriage. They use the word "shivaree" to mean "everyone get out from in front of the television, visit, and have a good time."

This event, attended by about 3,000, features arts and crafts, live entertainment, games, food booths, fun runs, and live music. Gatesville native Johnny Gimble and the Dick Gimble Band play the festival just about every year.

Moody
Junefest
First Saturday in June
Moody Chamber of Commerce, P.O. Box 419, Moody 76557, call City of Moody, 817/853-2314
Admission: free

Moody celebrates the green month of June with a parade, arts and crafts fair, barbecue cook-off, a pie baking contest, music all day by local bands, and a variety of games for kids and grown ups.

Waxahachie
The Gingerbread Trail Tour of Homes
First weekend in June
Waxahachie Chamber of Commerce, P.O. Box 187, Waxahachie 75165, 903/937-2390
Admission: $10 adult

The tour includes six historic homes and three museums, but that's not all there is to see. Waxahachie boasts a town square with every building listed in the National Register of

Historic Places.

You can take a tour bus that visits places seen in the many films shot in the Waxahachie area, including the Bethel Community, where parts of *Places in the Heart* were filmed. Other activities include a street dance on Saturday night, contests, arts and crafts, a stage show, and food booths.

Early
Annual Early Founders Day
First weekend in June
Early Chamber of Commerce, P.O. Box 3010, Early 76803, 915/643-5218
Admission: free

Founders Day takes place on the grounds of Heartland Mall, the largest shopping mall in a small town in Texas. Outdoor activities include a horse show, and horseshoe, washer, and golf pitching tournaments. Indoors you'll find arts and craft booths, a senior citizen domino tournament, antique tractor display, contests, and food booths.

Grand Saline
Salt Festival
Second weekend in June
Grand Saline Chamber of Commerce, P.O. Drawer R, Grand Saline 75410, 903/962-3555

Grand Saline means "big salt" in Spanish, and the folks in this town hold a festival in appreciation of the great salt deposit underground that's always played a part in their history.

The Cherokee Indians obtained salt by evaporating water from a salt marsh that lies over the salt dome. Settlers did the same thing by boiling the marsh water in kettles.

Later, entrepreneurs drilled shallow wells for salt brine and used large shallow pans for evaporation. Today Morton Salt operates a rock salt mine 750 feet below the surface. The salt dome itself is 20,000 feet tall and 1.5 miles in diameter at one point. Trucks and conveyor belts remove the salt, leaving large, hollowed-out "rooms."

The festival features a parade, dance, arts and crafts, a rodeo, a fiddling contest, and live entertainment. While you're in town, you can see the salt palace, the only building in the United States built entirely of salt. Of course a corrugated awning stands over the little house to protect it from the eroding effects of rain.

A boy gets soaked by a water balloon during kiddie games at the Grand Saline Salt Festival. Photo by Jack McNickle of the *Grand Saline Sun*.

Wichita Falls
Falls Fest
Second weekend in June
Wichita Falls Chamber of Commerce, P.O. Box 1860, Wichita Falls 76307, 817/723-2741
Admission: $3 to $4

This family event takes place in Lucy Park, where the waterfall is. Attractions include big name and local musical entertainment all three days, handmade arts and crafts for sale, food booths, a carnival, a fun run, and a bicycle ride.

For kids, there's a special recreation area and games, including a cookie eating contest.

Sulphur Springs
Ice Cream Freeze-Off and Dairy Festival
Second full week in June
Hopkins County Chamber of Commerce, P.O. Box 347, Sulphur Springs 75842, 903/885-6515
Admission: free

The Ice Cream Freeze-Off, sponsored by the Agricultural Extension Service on Saturday, draws contestants from far and wide to churn their frozen delights for the honor of the winning title. Flavors vary from the basic to the exotic, and visitors get to taste the creations for free after the judging.

Other activities include a parade, dairy-related arts and crafts show, contests, food booths and a dairy cattle show.

Pilot Point
Pioneer Days
Third weekend in June
Pilot Point Chamber of Commerce, P.O. Box 497, Pilot Point 76258, 817/686-5385
Admission: free

The Ugly Pickup Truck Contest may be the most interesting aspect of this event. Contestants pay an entry fee, park their ugly truck on the town square and wait anxiously for the judges' decision.

"We get some ugly ones, too," said Shirley Cannon of the chamber of commerce.

Other attractions include a Saturday parade, a Friday night dance, contests, a flea market, arts and crafts, food booths, and an old-time fiddler's contest. You can also enjoy a rodeo, mock bank robbery, and fire pumper races.

Hillsboro
Bond's Alley Art Festival
Second Sunday in June
Hillsboro Chamber of Commerce, P.O. Box 358, Hillsboro 76645, 817/582-2481
Admission: free

This festival began as a fundraiser for a city library, and now helps support the arts, historical preservation, and other community projects.

It features a dance, arts and crafts, a stage show, food booths, a courtyard cafe, an auction, fun run, tour of homes, petting zoo, trolley rides, and historic buildings open to the public.

Mount Vernon
Aquafest
First weekend in June
Franklin County Chamber of Commerce, P.O. Box 554, Mount Vernon 75457, 903/537-4365
Admission: free

Celebrating Lake Cypress Springs, this festival includes a parade, contests, ski show, diving tournament, skydiving, sports tournaments, children's games, arts and crafts, a stage show, and food booths. It's held at Guthrie Park on Lake Cypress Springs.

Munday
Knox County Vegetable Festival
Third weekend in June of even-numbered years
Munday Chamber of Commerce and Agriculture, P.O. Drawer L, Munday 76371, 817/422-4540
Admission: free

Known as the Vegetable Capital of North Texas, Knox County celebrates its varied produce with this event. Some of the primary crops are potatoes, onions, cucumbers, cabbage, cantaloupe and watermelon.

You'll find a farmer's market, vegetable judging and a contest in which people make faces and other forms out of vegetables. Home gardeners participate with a flower show and a home canning competition. Other attractions include the arts and crafts fair, stage show, and food booths.

Mineral Wells
Crazy Water Festival

Third weekend in June
Mineral Wells Chamber of Commerce, P.O. Box 393, Mineral Wells 76067, 817/325-2557
Admission: free

The Crazy Water Festival gets its name from the mineral water that made the city a leading health resort in the early 1900s. In those days, hotels offering mineral baths abounded not only in town, but also in other parts of the county.

The first well in the area was drilled by a settler, James Lynch, in 1877. His wife, who suffered from rheumatism, is said to have been cured by the water. After a public well was drilled in town, a mentally ill woman who drank of it became her old self again, as the story goes. So well water of the area was coined Crazy Water and became famous nationwide for its curative qualities.

Now, all the mineral wells are capped but one, inside the building of the Famous Water Company, which still sells Crazy Water.

The festival features a 10K run, bike rally, volksmarch, arts and crafts, live entertainment, a community theatre performance, and food booths.

Jacksboro
Weekend in Old Mesquiteville
Second weekend in June
Jacksboro Chamber of Commerce, P.O. Box 606, Jacksboro 76056, 817/567-2602
Admission: free

This festival begins when horseback riders from Old Fort Richardson State Park ride into town, parade around the square and fire a cannon. Other activities include several bike races: 100-mile, 65-mile, 35-mile, 25-mile and the 5-mile Little Smokie.

A dance, an arts and crafts fair, a melodrama, cloggers, singing, and wagon rides also entertain visitors. You can visit nearby Fort Richardson State Historical Park. This fort was the northernmost of federal frontier forts built after the Civil War.

Bowie
Jim Bowie Days
Last weekend in June
Bowie Chamber of Commerce, 115 E. Tarrant, Bowie 76230, 817/872-1173
Admission: free; fees for rodeo, dances

This starts on Thursday with a parade, barbecue and gospel singing. Friday features kids games. Saturday you'll find arts and crafts exhibits, various contests, food, and a fiddler's contest. Other activities include rodeo for three nights and dances on Friday and Saturday nights.

Decatur
Chisolm Trail Days and Fun Run
Last Saturday in June
Decatur Chamber of Commerce, P.O. Box 474, Decatur 76234, 817/627-3107
Admission: free

The Chisolm Trail, which cattle drivers followed to Kansas in the late 1800s, is said to have passed near Decatur. The cattle drives from Texas to railroads farther north helped bring Texas out of financial hard times. One trail led from Fort Worth, passing Decatur on the east on its way to Red River Station, the official intersection with the Chisolm Trail on the Red River.

Now, the people of Decatur celebrate this legacy with a parade, dance, barbecue meal, 5K and 10K runs, an arts and crafts fair, and food booths.

New Boston
Pioneer Days and Rodeo
Last weekend in June
New Boston Chamber of Commerce, 303 E. North Front, New Boston 75570, 903/628-2581
Admission: free; fees for some events

New Boston remembers its heritage with a parade, dances and entertainment. One unique event is the men's beauty pageant, held on Thursday night. Most of the men dress up to look like beautiful women in serious evening gowns, but some, dressed in hilarious get-ups, send the audience into fits of laughter.

Activities include an arts and crafts fair, street and rodeo dances, music, a pancake breakfast, a barbecue supper, flea market, saloon show, and games.

New Boston lies within a few miles of towns called Boston and Old Boston. This confusing geographical name game started in the early 1800s, when settlers first came to northeast Texas from the United States.

These people named their town Boston, and in 1840 it became the county seat of Bowie County.

In 1876, the first railroad through the county missed Boston by about four miles, prompting everyone to pick up and move closer to the railroad. The new settlement, made up mostly of the same people, was called New Boston, and Boston eventually became a ghost town.

In 1885, the county seat was moved to Texarkana, a much bigger city, but not in the center of the county. People fussed for several years over the proper location of the courthouse, with all kinds of haggling and fighting and stealing of the county records. Finally, they put the county seat in the geographical center of the county, which happened to be halfway between Boston and New Boston.

By this time, the original Boston was just about empty, but still had an old post office the government wasn't using. So, they moved the post office to the new county seat and named the new place Boston. Then they named the original Boston Old Boston.

Noonday
Noonday Onion Festival
Second Saturday in June
Tyler Chamber of Commerce, 407 N. Broadway, Tyler 75703, 903/592-1661
Admission: $1

Noonday, a little bitty town outside Tyler, is famous for growing the world's sweetest, most delicious onions. You've probably heard of those onions from Vadalia, Georgia and Walla Walla, Washington that are supposed to be sweet. But they're nothing compared to the original Noonday Onion.

Activities include an arts and crafts fair, which features a special area of arts and crafts from East Texas, an onion growers competition, food booths, a country kitchen, fresh sweet onion rings, live music, and children's games.

Two popular events are the bald man and bald baby contests. Whoever has the shiniest head and looks the most like an onionhead wins. In the tear-jerker storytelling contest, storytellers try to make the judges cry with a story while peeling an onion. If you buy a bushel of the bulbs, they'll hold them for you while you wander around the festival grounds.

★

Randy Dickens of Fairfield competes in the peach pit spitting during Fairfield's Peach Festival. Photo courtesy *The Fairfield Recorder.*

JULY

Timpson
Frontier Days
First weekend in July
Timpson Chamber of Commerce, P.O. Box 339, Timpson 75975, call *Timpson-Tenaha News* at 409/254-3618
Admission: $3

Most everyone in Timpson comes out for Frontier Days to enjoy a parade, street dance, rodeo, arts and crafts, food, music, and a variety of games.

Fairfield
Peach Festival
July 4
Fairfield Chamber of Commerce, P.O. Box 956, Fairfield 75840, 903/389-5792
Admission: free

Since peaches are a major crop in the Fairfield area, the folks there get together each July 4 for an old-fashioned picnic revolving around the sweet, juicy peach.

They have peach ice cream, horseshoe pitching, singing, an arts and crafts fair, a sack race, fireworks display and an antique car show.

Peach experts judge the local crop, then the fruit is auctioned off. A peach cooking competition turns up all kinds of yummy peach dishes. And of course, don't forget the peach ice cream freeze-off and the pit-spitting contest.

Mineola
Freedomfest
July 4
Mineola Chamber of Commerce, P.O. Box 68, Mineola 75773, 903/569-2087
Admission: free

Mineola celebrates July 4 with a fireworks display, fun run, volleyball tournament, tennis tournament, dunking booth, horseshoe tournament and bingo. There's also live entertainment, arts and crafts and food booths.

Ore City
Ore City Fourth of July Fun Festival
July 4

City of Ore City, P.O. Box 327, Ore City 75863, 903/968-2511

Iron ore used to be a big industry in northeast Texas, where you'll see older houses built of a reddish stone, surrounded by the sandy red soil.

This small town's Independence Day celebration features a parade, dance, arts and crafts fair, fireworks display, food booths, and games for kids and grown-ups.

If you're looking for a workout, they have a 5K run, one-mile walk, and bicycle races. About 1,200 people turn out for the festivities.

Stephenville
July 4th Family Fun Fair
July 4
Stephenville Chamber of Commerce, P.O. Box 306, Stephenville 76401, 817/965-5313
Admission: free

After a long day of celebration, Stephenville's community choir performs patriotic numbers in the evening before the fireworks display. Daytime events include a parade, a greased pig catch, and live entertainment all day on two stages. There's also an arts and crafts fair, food booths, and a variety of games.

Bridgeport
Butterfield Stage Days
Second weekend in July
Bridgeport Chamber of Commerce, P.O. Box 1104, Bridgeport 76026, 817/683-2076
Admission: free except for barbecue

Bridgeport got its name from the toll bridge built for the Butterfield Stagecoach line over the West Fork of the Trinity River. The town grew up around the stagecoach stop, and remained even after the stage quit running during the Civil War.

The festival begins on Saturday with outdoor contests, a carnival, entertainment in the park, food booths and arts and crafts. Games include horseshoes, washers and something special for the kids. They usually have stagecoach rides as well. At night you can partake of the barbecue supper, then attend the street dance. A rodeo parade takes place the next Thursday, followed by three days of rodeo.

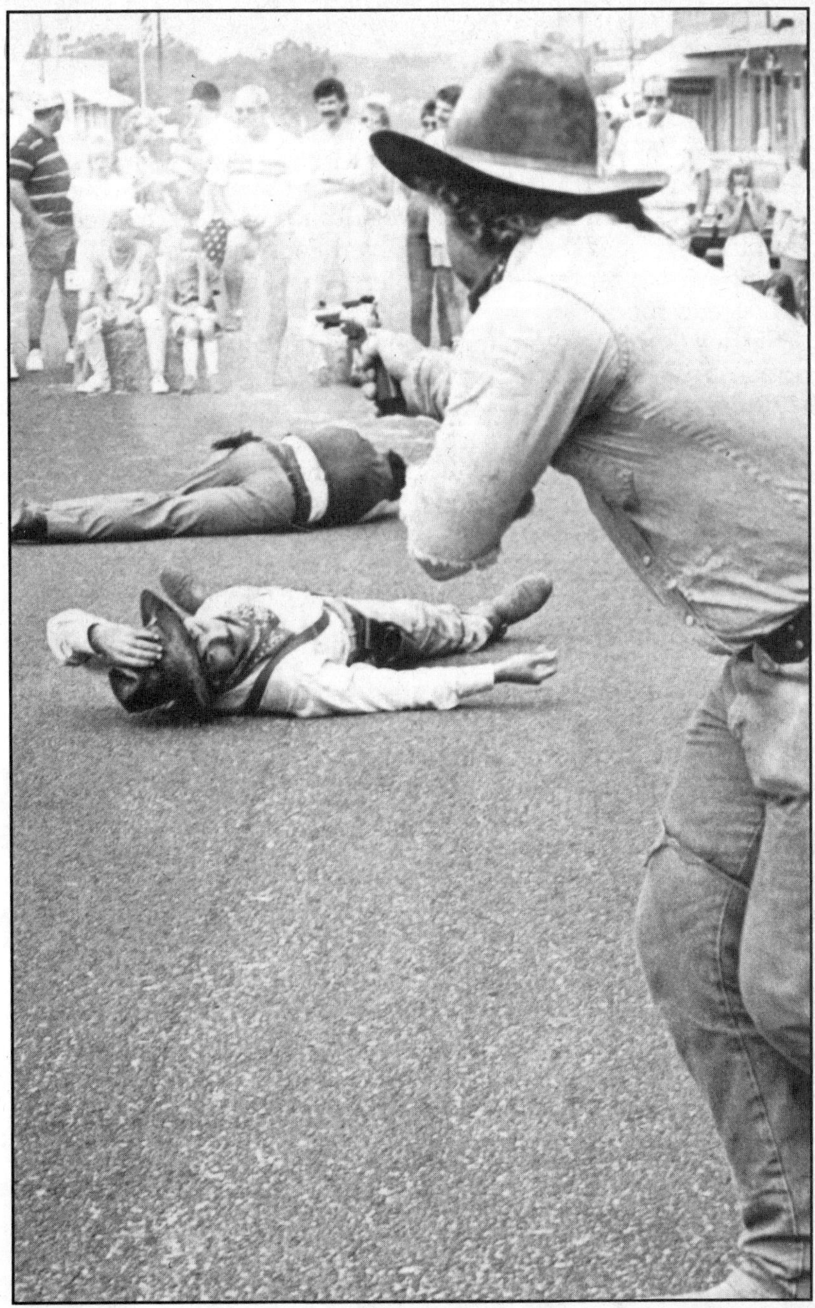

The Crack in the Wall Gang performs a shootout during Butterfield Stage Days in Bridgeport. *Bridgeport Index* Photo by Joann Pritchard.

Lampasas
Spring Ho Festival
Second weekend in July
Lampasas County Chamber of Commerce, P.O. Box 627, Lampasas 76550, 512/556-5172
Admission: free; fees for some events

Lampasas grew up around two sulphur springs that feed a tributary creek of the Colorado River. Each year this Hill Country town remembers its waters with a festival of music, games and food.

Shirley Swinney, secretary of the Spring Ho Committee, said of the springs that feed Sulphur Creek, "They're sulphur springs, and when the weather's right they really smell."

"People used to come here and take 'the cure.' We were known as the Saratoga of the South," she said. "They figured anything that bad-smelling had to be good for you."

Most of the festival takes place in a park just downstream from one of the springs, and you can walk over to see it. Activities really start during the week, with most of the action on Saturday and Sunday.

During the week they have a fireworks display, gospel singing, a children's fishing contest, and a horse show. Friday is full of activities for children like the diaper derby, pet parade, a magician, and face painting. There's also a street dance Friday night.

Saturday features the parade, 10K and 1 mile runs, barbecue cook-off, antique car show, gardener's harvest market, petting zoo and music on the bandstand all afternoon. An arts and crafts fair and food concessions round out the festivities on both Saturday and Sunday.

The U.S. Army Band from Fort Hood, the Startzville Stompers, the Sahawe Indian Dancers, a water sports demonstration, and a nighttime street dance entertain visitors Saturday. Sunday attractions consist of an old time fiddler's contest, the Indian Dancers and the Austin Civic Wind Ensemble.

Paris
Bastille Days Celebration
Weekend closest to July 14
Paris Visitor and Convention Center, 1651 Clarksville, Paris 75460, 903/784-2501
Admission: free

In honor of the big Paris in France, the folks in this Red

River town throw a festival commemorating the day French peasants stormed the Bastille, a major turning point in the French Revolution. In France, Bastille Day is much like our Independence Day.

They have an antique auto parade, a street dance, artist display, tour de Paris bike race, French film festival, community theatre performance, municipal band concert, plenty of food concessions and old-fashioned children's games on the lawn of a historic home.

Weatherford
Parker County Peach Festival
Second Saturday in July
Weatherford Chamber of Commerce, P.O. Box 310, Weatherford 76086, 817/594-3801
Admission: free

About 9,000 people show up for this festival, which features a peach ice cream freeze-off and peach cooking competition. Other events include a 25-mile bicycle ride, 10K run, biathlon, old- time fiddler's contest, 42 tournament, and barbecue dinner. There's plenty of live entertainment, food booths, and an arts and crafts fair. Weatherford peach farmers grow seven varieties of the fruit.

Athens
Black-eyed Pea Jamboree
Third weekend in July
Athens Chamber of Commerce, P.O. Box 2600, Athens 75751, 903/675-5181
Admission: free; fee to some events

Athens, known as the Black-eyed Pea Capital of the World, celebrates the nutritious, luck-enhancing legume with three days of food, fun and entertainment. This festival attracts about 30,000 visitors throughout the weekend.

Plenty of food is available, including various black-eyed pea dishes. Visitors can take part in pea shelling, pea eating, and pea popping contests. Other activities include a parade, a pea cook-off, a bike tour, the Miss Black-Eyed Pea pageant, an arts and crafts fair, carnival, musical entertainment, and a watermelon eating contest.

Wylie
July Jubilee
Third weekend in July

Wylie Chamber of Commerce, Box 918, Wylie 75098, 903/442-2804
Admission: free

The July Jubilee offers a parade, street dance, gospel singing, and a carnival. The street dance, usually held on Saturday night, is a favorite of many townspeople. When the sun goes down, folks bring their folding chairs downtown to hear the Wylie Opry House Band play and watch their friends dance the night away.

Hico
Hico Old Settler's Reunion
Fourth week in July
Hico Civic Club, P.O. Box 93, Hico 76457, City of Hico, 817/796-4620
Admission: free

This celebration began in 1883 and now attracts a crowd of 10,000. Fesivities include a parade, dance, arts and crafts fair, fun run, music, and food.

Naples
Watermelon Festival and Rodeo
Last Thursday, Friday and Saturday in July
Naples Chamber of Commerce, P.O. Box 55096, Naples 75568, 903/897-5931
Admission: free

A friendly get together in Naples provides free watermelon for everyone Saturday afternoon. Other activities include a parade, trail ride, street dance, fun run, rodeo, food booths, all-day live music, arts and crafts, horseshoes, bingo, and an antique car contest.

★

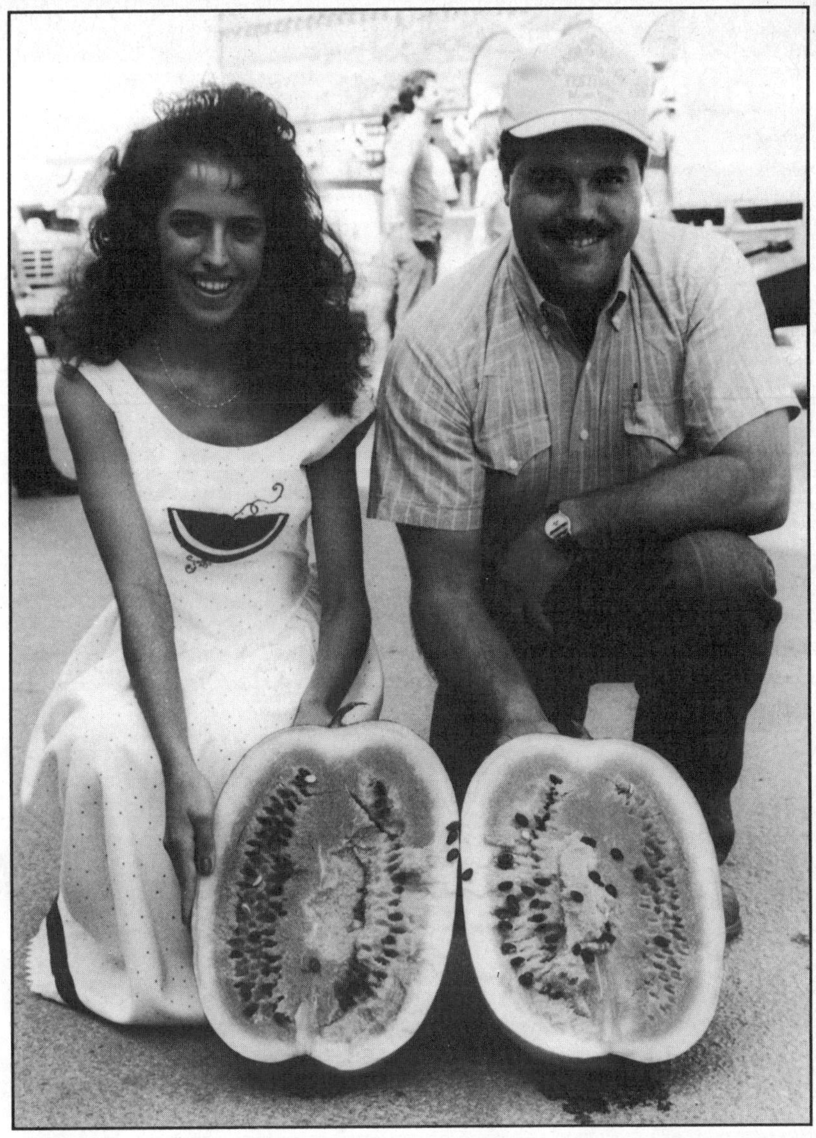

De Leon Peach and Melon Festival Queen Shelli Hammit and chairman Joey Mahan display a melon to be eaten during the free melon slicing. Photo courtesy *DeLeon Free Press.*

AUGUST

De Leon
De Leon Peach and Melon Festival
First full week of August
De Leon Chamber of Commerce, 404 Navarro, DeLeon 76444, 817/893-2083
Admission: $1

Since 1924, the people of DeLeon have honored their fruit crop with the Peach and Melon Festival. About 31,000 attend the festivities, which feature a parade, dance, arts and crafts, live entertainment and food booths. Watermelon events include melon judging, a seed spitting contest, a free watermelon feed, and auction of prize melons.

Paris
Northeast Texas Heritage Festival
Second weekend in August
Paris Junior College, 2400 Clarksville, Paris 75460, Johnye Robertson, 903/785-9574
For accommodations info: Lamar County Chamber of Commerce, P.O. Box 1096, Paris 75460, 903/784-2501
Admission: free

This historically-oriented festival on the campus of Paris Junior College offers craft demonstrations, storytelling, and music, all drawn from days gone by. Demonstrations include spinning, weaving, butter churning, operation of a grist mill, and woodworking, among other skills. A barbecue meal satisfies visitors' appetites, and wagon rides provide more recreation.

In honor of Dr. William Owens, author of 18 books on Texas music and folklore, a musical based on his collected works is performed. Owens, an alumnus of Paris Junior College, has recorded the music and stories of northeast Texas, as well as other parts of the state. His best-known book is probably *This Stubborn Soil.*

Denton
North Texas State Fair
One week in August
Denton Convention and Visitors Bureau, P.O. Drawer P, Denton 76202, 817/382-7895
Admission: $2 to $4

This fair features a parade, country and western street dances, an arts and crafts fair, live music, a rodeo, and chili, bean and barbecue cook-offs.

Atlanta
Forest Festival
Third weekend in August
Atlanta Area Chamber of Commerce, P.O. Box 29, Atlanta 75551, 903/796-3296
Admission: free

This five-day event inspired by the forested, rolling hills of the Atlanta area features a parade, lumberjack contests, an arts and crafts fair, live entertainment, food booths, games, a beauty pageant, a classic car show, and carnival rides.

Wichita Falls
Texas Ranch Roundup
Third weekend in August
Wichita Falls Chamber of Commerce, P.O. Box 1860, Wichita Falls 76307, 817/723-2741
Admission: $4 adult

Cowboys from the state's major ranches compete to see who's best at roping, branding, wild cow milking, and other ranching tasks. This is not competition for money, but for the honor of being judged the most skilled team of cowboys.

Other activities include dances and cowboy cooking competition.

SEPTEMBER

West
Westfest
Labor Day weekend
Westfest, Inc. P.O. Box 65, West 76691, 817/826-5058
Admission: $4 per day adult

One of the largest ethnic culture festivals in the state, Westfest offers food, music and dancing to travelers out for Labor Day weekend. Celebrating Czech heritage, about 35,000 people attend this celebration, which serves to protect the rich culture so many Texans are part of.

Mandy Mikulencak wrote in *Texas Highways* in August 1988 that the first Czechoslovakian immigrants to Texas came in the 1850s. Texas now has the largest rural Czech population in the United States, and the largest Czech population in the South.

When the Czechs left their homeland in the 1850s, it wasn't yet called Czechoslovakia as a nation, but was part of the Austro-Hungarian Empire. There were four regions: Bohemia, Moravia, Silesia and and Slovakia. When you hear Texans talk about "Bohemians," they're probably referring to descendants of Czech settlers.

Oppression of Czech culture by the Austro-Hungarian government led many Czechs to leave when the escape door opened in the 1850s. They settled in much of Central and South Central Texas, bringing with them their religion, food, family traditions and music.

Westfest includes lots of dancing, with many well-known polka bands and two dancing areas. For food, there's sausage, sauerkraut, kolaches (sweet rolls made with fruit) and strudel. If you've never had a poppyseed kolache, try one at Westfest.

Besides the dancing areas, there's a cultural tent featuring entertainment from other ethnic groups inlcuding Norwegian, Mexican, Ukrainian and Polish. Other attractions include Sokol gymnastics demonstration, a parade, an arts and crafts fair, games, and a large children's area.

Celina
Fun Day
Second weekend in September
Celina Chamber of Commerce, P.O. Box 387, Celina 75009, 903/382-2108

Celina's townspeople get together this day to enjoy a parade, dance, arts and crafts fair, and bicycle and foot races. There's plenty of music, games and food.

Hewitt
Hewitt Hay Daze
Second Saturday in September
Greater Hewitt Chamber of Commerce, P.O. Box 661, Hewitt 76643, 817/666-1200
Admission: free; $1 for dance

Begun in 1978, Hay Daze now draws 5,000 people and includes a street dance, free entertainment throughout the day, live music, waiter races, contests, arts and crafts, and food booths. The children's area features pony rides, stagecoach rides, games, and a treasure hunt.

Commerce
Bois d'Arc Bash
Second weekend in September
Commerce Chamber of Commerce, P.O. Box 290, Commerce 75429, 903/886-3950
Admission: free

This festival, named after the horseapple or Osage Orange tree, started in 1985 to honor Commerce's 100th birthday. Activities include a dance, contests, all-day musical entertainment, exhibits of items made from bois d'arc trees, arts and crafts, and food booths.

Bois d'arc is prized for its hardness and durability. The word bois d'arc is French for "wood of the bow." The tree got this name because the Osage Indians used the wood to make their bows. Back in the olden days, you couldn't get a house loan in some parts of Central Texas unless the building sat on bois d'arc piers, according to Paul Cox and Patty Leslie in their book *Texas Trees*. That's how durable and resistant to rot the wood is. It was also used for wagon wheel hubs.

Denton
County Seat Saturday
Second weekend in September
Denton Convention and Visitors Bureau, P.O. Drawer P, 414 Parkway, Denton 76202, 817/382-7895
Admission: free

Denton celebrates its status as county seat with a children's hat parade, old-fashioned games, arts and crafts exhibits and sales, and food booths. Entertainment includes a variety of music from country to rock, Wild West shows, dancers, bed races, and stagecoach rides.

Sulphur Springs
World Champion Hopkins County Stew Contest and Fall Festival
Second and third weekends in September
Hopkins County Chamber of Commerce, P.O. Box 347, Sulphur Springs 75482, 903/885-6515
Admission to some events; you can buy a ticket that allows you to sample all the stews

Traditionally, Hopkins County Stew is made with chicken, and nobody has ever won the cook-off with anything else. The cook-off takes place the second Saturday of the festival, with cooks stirring their stew in large kettles over open fires.

Jodie Morris, manager of the tourism and visitors bureau, said most of the contestants enter the costume and site competition as well as the cooking. You'll see plenty of people who look like they stepped out of an East Texas log cabin.

Visitors are invited to enjoy the ample amount of stew. "You buy a ticket, and you can eat stew till you can't stand it," Morris said. Cheese, crackers and pickles are included in the ticket price.

Another unique event during the fall festival is the Cover Girl Contest. This is not a beauty pageant. The girls have to do more than play the piano or twirl a baton. Each contestant must drive a tractor, milk a cow, pluck a chicken, sew something, and rope a calf, among other things. The contest goes on all week, with different events each night, ending when the winner is crowned Saturday afternoon.

Other activities during the two weekends and week include a parade, a street dance, a large arts and crafts fair, a local talent show outdoors, food booths, and a carnival.

Gorman
Peanut Festival
Third Saturday in September
Gorman Chamber of Commerce, P.O. Box 266, Gorman 76454, 817/734-3110
Admission: free

With two major peanut companies, Gorman is the Peanut Capital of the Southwest. Their Peanut Festival was reborn in 1985 after a 20-year lapse. Gormanites celebrate their main industry with a parade, game booths, a dance, contests, arts and crafts, food booths and a stage show.

They have a peanut bake-off, in which all entries, whether pies, cakes or cookies, must contain some form of peanuts. You'll find all types of peanut treats for sale, too. Kids can compete in peanut rolling and tossing contests.

Malakoff
Lakefest
Third weekend in September
Malakoff Chamber of Commerce, P.O. Box 1042, Malakoff 75148, 903/489-1518
Admission: free

Malakoff, near Cedar Creek Lake, puts together a bluegrass show, sailboat races, a golf tournament, a parade, contests, an arts and crafts fair, and food booths.

Springtown
Wild West Festival
Third Saturday in September
Springtown Chamber of Commerce, P.O. Box 296, Springtown 76082, 817/523-7828
Admission: free

Springtown looks back to the early days of Texas with a parade, old-time fiddler's contest, live music, arts and crafts and food booths. There's a best-dressed contest, a group that performs mock gunfights, country games, and other entertainment.

Hillsboro
Cotton Pickin' Fair
Third weekend in September
Hillsboro Chamber of Commerce, P.O. Box 358, Hillsboro 76645, 817/582-2481
Admission: free

To celebrate the agricultural heritage of the Hillsboro area, local citizens organize heritage arts demonstrations, an antique and modern farm equipment exhibit and automobile exhibit. They also host a fun run, sidewalk sale, antique sale and show, tours of historic buildings, a dance, contests, a stage show, and food booths.

Pittsburg
Pioneer Days

Third weekend in September
Camp County Chamber of Commerce, 202 Jefferson, Pittsburg 75686, 903/856-3442
Admission: free

In honor of Pittsburg's pioneers and founders, the town puts together a parade, dance, contests, antique car show, arts and crafts booths, stage show and food booths. Pioneer Days started in 1973 and now attracts 15,000 people each year.

Athens
Uncle Fletch Davis Home of the Hamburger Cook-off and Trade Fair
Fourth Saturday in September
Athens Chamber of Commerce, P.O. Box 2600, Athens 75751, 903/675-5181
Admission: free

Texas is famous for chili, barbecue and pecan pie. But one food you wouldn't ordinarily think of as coming from Texas was invented in Athens.

That's right, the hamburger was unknown to the world outside Athens, Texas, until 1904, when Fletcher Davis journeyed to the St. Louis World's Fair to sell hamburgers on the midway. A native of Webster Groves, Missouri, near St. Louis, Davis moved to Athens when he was young and worked at the Athens/Miller Pottery, according to the late Frank Tolbert in *Tolbert's Texas*. Later, Davis opened a cafe on the town square, where he served a ground beef sandwich.

In 1904, the *New York Tribune* ran a story about a new sandwich at the World's Fair. Although the story didn't mention who made the sandwich, a nephew of Fletch Davis told Tolbert he remembered going to the World's Fair to visit his uncle, and seeing his hamburger booth.

Activities include the hamburger cook-off, a street dance, athletic events, live entertainment, a carnival, an artisan fair, and a domino tournament.

Comanche
Comanche County Pow-wow
Fourth weekend in September
Comanche Chamber of Commerce, P.O. Box 65, Comanche 76442, 915/356-3233
Admission: $1

Two days of family fun await you in Comanche. The festival features an arts and crafts fair, music by the U.S. Army Band

and western bands, muzzleloader demonstrations, a street dance, and a brisket cook-off. Other entertainment includes Indian dancers, square dancers, and singers.

You can see an old car show, a photography show, and dog trials. Games include peanut guessing and egg toss.

Jacksonville
Tomato Fest
Fourth weekend in September
Jacksonville Chamber of Commerce, P.O. Box 1231, Jacksonville 75766, 903/586-2217
Admission: $1 adult

In the 1930s and 1940s, Jacksonville shipped out more tomatoes than any other community in the United States. In fact, many packing and shipping methods in use today were developed in Jacksonville.

To remember those days, the townspeople celebrate with tomato events, a handcrafted arts and crafts fair, barbecue cook-off, and an 8K run. Games include horseshoe and washer pitching.

In the Couch Tomato Competition/No Sweat Olympics, people try their hand at tomato pool, tomato golf, and tomato basketball. The Battle of San Tomato pits teams against each other in a timed obstacle course.

Held at the Cherokee County Fairgrounds, this event attracts about 7,000 people.

Texarkana
Quadrangle Festival
Fourth Saturday in September
Texarkana Chamber of Commerce, P.O. Box 1468, Texarkana 75594, 903/792-7191
Admission: $1

This event attracts people to the downtown area with historic crafts demonstrations, live music, arts and crafts, and food booths. The music usually includes country, gospel, pop, and rock, with at least one well-known band. There are also 5K and 10K runs.

Farmersville
Old Time Saturday
Last Saturday of September or first Saturday of October
Farmersville Chamber of Commerce, P.O. Box 366, Farmersville 75031, 903/782-6234

Admission: $1

Since 1974, Farmersville has raised money for its library and community center with this festival. Everyone dresses up in "old-time" clothing for this one-day event that features stagecoach rides, gunfights, a watermelon eating contest, a cow chip throwing contest, a square dance, barbecue dinner, dance, and food booths.

Buffalo
Annual Buffalo Stampede
Last Saturday in September
Buffalo Chamber of Commerce, P.O. Box 207, Buffalo 75831, 903/322-5810
Admission: free

The Stampede features a parade, dance, arts and crafts fair, a 42 tournament, horseshoe toss, and watermelon seed-spitting contest. There's a barbecue meal and chili cook-off. Entertainment varies from year to year, but they always have games for children.

Hawkins
Hawkins Oil Festival
Last weekend in September or first weekend in October
Hawkins Chamber of Commerce, Box 345, Hawkins 75765, 903/769-3517
Admission: free

The oil boom came to Hawkins in 1940, and the Exxon plant still exists as the backbone of the town's economy. The folks come out to celebrate the petroleum industry and the soil from which the liquid comes with the Oil Festival.

Activities include a parade, trail ride, an arts and crafts fair, and entertainment. There's usually plenty of food to eat, too.

★

OCTOBER

Longview
Loblolly Jubilee
First weekend in October
Longview Convention and Visitors Bureau, 100 Grand Blvd., Longview 75604, 903/753-3281
Admission: $2 adult

Large and beautiful loblolly pines give East Texas its characteristic look and feel. The trees enhance the lives of the people there with their shade, beauty, and value as timber.

Longview pays tribute to the tree with a street dance, fun run, forestry exhibits, an arts and crafts fair, a civil war encampment, food, an antique car show, chili and barbecue cook-offs, and a carnival.

In the professional lumberjack show, real lumberjacks demonstrate log rolling, chopping, sawing and other skills combined with a comedy routine.

The Largest Loblolly contest challenges people to find the largest loblolly pine in the county.

Whitney
Pioneer Days
First Saturday in October
Lake Whitney Chamber of Commerce, P.O. Box 604, Whitney 76692, 817/694-2540
Admission: free; fee for street dance

Near Lake Whitney, this town puts on a down home fall festival. This area is a nice place to be in the fall, especially for camping.

They have a parade, dance, arts and crafts fair, usually a bicycle race, a baby contest, horseshoe tournament, food, live entertainment all day, and a tour of homes.

Winnsboro
Autumn Trails
Each weekend in October
Winnsboro Chamber of Commerce, 201 W. Broadway, Winnsboro 75494, 903/342-3666
Admission: free

Northeast Texas is beautiful all the time, but it's just about the only area in Texas where you can see a "traditional" autumn with red and gold leaves among the pines.

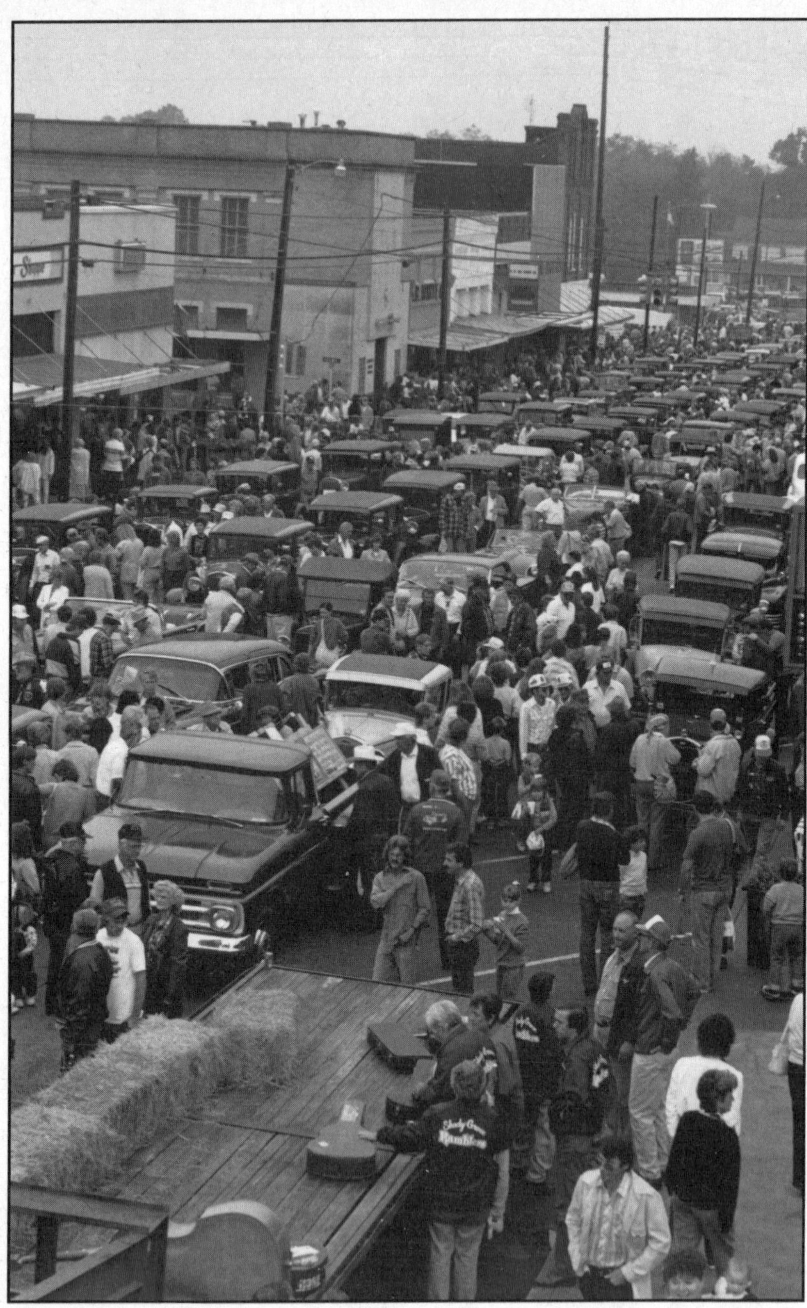

People and autos fill Winnsboro's Main Street during Antique Car Weekend of Winnsboro Autumn Trails. Photo courtesy *The Winnsboro News.*

The Winnsboro area glows in the autumn, and the folks there are proud of it. They show off their forests with several backroad auto tours, maps of which can be obtained in town. These make nice bicycle outings, too.

There's something happening in town each weekend during October. Activities include a trail ride, parade, barn and square dances, contests, an arts and crafts fair, a trade day, antique car show, bass tournament, golf tournament, and chili cook-off. Events are scheduled differently each year, so contact the chamber of commerce to find out what happens when.

Center
East Texas Poultry Festival
First Thursday, Friday and Saturday in October
Shelby County Chamber of Commerce, 321 Shelbyville St., Center 75935, 409/598-3682
Admission: $2 button covers whole weekend

This is Center's main event of the year, focusing on the poultry industry, a mainstay of the East Texas economy. Activities include chicken judging and auction, musical entertainment, a carnival, a dance, an arts and crafts fair, food booths, and craft and canning competitions.

Colleyville
Colleyville Barbecue Cook-off
Early October
Colleyville Chamber of Commerce, P.O. Box 445, Colleyville 76034, 817/488-7148
Admission: free

Organized by the Colleyville Barbecue Association, this festival has a parade, street dance, contests, food booths, children's area and, of course, a barbecue cook-off. The cook-off is for beef, sausage, ribs, or whatever.

Eastland
Old Rip Fest
First Saturday in October
Eastland Chamber of Commerce, 102 S. Seaman, Eastland 76448, 817/629-2332
Admission: free

This event pays homage to a horned toad who lived in the cornerstone of the Eastland County Courthouse for 31 years. When the courthouse was built in 1897, Justice of the Peace Earnest Wood put the horned toad in the cornerstone with a

Bible and other objects. The courthouse was torn down in February 1928, and 3,000 people gathered to see if the toad still lived in the cornerstone. Much to their surprise, he was alive.

They named him Old Rip and took him on a tour of the United States, which included a visit to President Calvin Coolidge. But, the travel must have worn him down, for Old Rip died of pneumonia in January, 1929, less than a year after his release from the cornerstone. Now, his little stuffed amphibian body lies in a casket in the courthouse lobby. You can see it through a window anytime.

The Old Rip Fest features a parade which sometimes includes toad-related floats, music, a fiddler's contest, tricycle races, a national marching band contest, a street dance, food booths and an arts and crafts fair. They also sell T-shirts that say "Old Rip Slept Here."

Nocona
Pow-Wow Peddle
First Saturday in October
Nocona Chamber of Commerce, P.O. Box 27, Nocona 76255, 817/825-3526

Since 1987, this town near the Red River has celebrated with a parade, contests, arts and crafts, stage show, and food booths.

Iowa Park
Whoop-T-Do
October or November, depending on the date of the homecoming football game
Iowa Park Chamber of Commerce, P.O. Box 146, Iowa Park 76367, 817/592-9553

Since 1970, Iowa Park has organized this big Whoop-T-Do, featuring a parade, variety of contests, arts and crafts, live bands and food booths. The homecoming football game is on Friday night, and most events are Saturday.

Marshall
East Texas Fireant Festival
Second weekend in October
Marshall Chamber of Commerce, P.O. Box 520, Marshall 75671, 903/935-7868
Admission: free

Fireants may be Texas' most-feared insects, with their ability to crawl in groups, unnoticed, onto a victim's leg, then deliver their stings all at once, as if given a signal by their leader.

People in Marshall show their respect for this formidable creature with a well-attended, lively festival. Activities include a parade, dance, a chili cook-off, 5K run, fireant calling contest, fireant roundup, fireant diaper derby, and the Tour de Fireant bicycle race. There's continuous entertainment during the day, and a street dance Saturday night.

Grapeland
Peanut Festival
Homecoming weekend, which is different each year
Houston County Chamber of Commerce, P.O. Box 307, Crockett 75835, 409/544-2359
Admission: free

Grapelanders organize a parade, arts and crafts fair, live music, carnival and food area. You'll find plenty of peanut food for sale.

Tyler
Texas Rose Festival
Weekend in mid-October
Tyler Chamber of Commerce, 407 N. Broadway, Tyler 75703, 903/592-1661
Admission: fee for some events

This festival features the world famous Tyler Rose Parade, an arts and crafts fair in the park, a rose show, tours of rose fields, and a dance.

Mineola
Heritage Arts Festival
Third Saturday in October
Mineola Chamber of Commerce, P.O. Box 68, Mineola 75773, 903/569-2087
Admission: free

The Heritage Arts Festival primarily includes demonstrations of the skills, crafts and way of life of pioneers. Townspeople don pioneer clothing for the occasion, set in historic Mineola. A wagon ride winds through the historical district, and all the food for sale is cooked the old-fashioned way. Visitors can see demonstrations of soap making, candle making, spinning, weaving, quilting and other things people used to do for themselves.

Other activities include a parade, story telling and music.

Gilmer
East Texas Yamboree
Third weekend in October
Upshur County Chamber of Commerce, P.O. Box 854, Gilmer 75644, 903/843-2413
Admission: free; fee for some events

This festival began in 1935 to salute the sweet potato, which was a major crop in the area in the 1930s, 40s and 50s. Although they call it the Yamboree, it's really the sweet potato they're celebrating. One of the most popular Texas festivals, the Yamboree attracts about 100,000 visitors.

Events include a parade, yam pie competition, the Yam Queen pageant, a street dance, foot race, bicycle tour, carnival, tennis tournament, art and photography shows, a livestock show, fiddler's contest, and barbecue meal.

Whitesboro
Peanut Festival
Third Saturday in October
Whitesboro Area Chamber of Commerce, P.O. Box 522, Whitesboro 76273, 903/564-3331
Admission: free

The Peanut Festival, celebrated since 1965, includes a parade, dance, contests, arts and crafts, talent contest, food booths, fun run, games, domino tournament, fiddler's contest and auction.

Daingerfield
Captain Daingerfield Day
Third weekend in October
Daingerfield Chamber of Commerce, 208 Jefferson, Daingerfield 75638, 903/645-2646

Daingerfield, the fourth oldest town in Texas, is named after Captain London Daingerfield, who came to Northeast Texas from Nova Scotia in the early 1800s.

The festival includes a chili cook-off, parade, street dance, arts and crafts, music, singing and food booths. Contests include the cow chip toss and the wild and wacky pumper races, in which teams race to see who can get a fire hose hooked up and running first.

"The fire department helped with the pumper races, and it was just hilarious, because there wasn't a dry person left at the end," said Peggy Maxey, secretary-manager of the Daingerfield Chamber of Commerce.

One year, to prepare for the cow chip toss, Maxey and the chamber president gathered cow chips from a neighbor's barn. "We went down and picked the good petrified ones out of the barn, and tried to get them all the same size so it would be fair," she explained.

They put the cow chips in a plastic garbage bag and set them in her front yard. But the morning before the contest, city garbage collectors, doing their duty, carried away the bag, leaving Maxey the job of gathering chips again.

Golden
Sweet Potato Festival
Fourth Saturday in October
Bob Hughes, Route 3 Box 229, Mineola 75773, 903/768-2353
Admission: free

Golden residents celebrate the sweet potato harvest with a parade, arts and crafts fair, and a 26-mile bike race through the beautiful fall foliage and rolling hills of the area. There's also a 4.9-kilometer foot race, games, a horseshoe tournament, a fiddler's contest, all-day musical entertainment, and wagon rides.

For the sweet potato auction, growers donate a box of potatoes, which are judged, then auctioned off as a fundraiser. There's also a sweet potato cooking contest with youth and adult divisions. Entries to the contest are also auctioned off.

Kaufman
Kaufman Scarecrow Festival
Last full week of October
Kaufman Chamber of Commerce, 112 S. Washington, Kaufman 75142, 903/932-3118
Admission: free

Celebrating the fall harvest, Kaufmanites host a scarecrow building contest, a pumpkin cook-off, and a parade as major events of the Scarecrow Festival.

Palestine
Five Alarm Hot Pepper Festival
Last weekend in October
Palestine Chamber of Commerce, P.O. Box 1177, Palestine 75802, 903/729-6066
Admission: free

They have a parade, dance, arts and crafts fair, wild game cook-off, fire department races, music, and lots of food to eat.

Palestine hosts the only annual fire department parade in Texas, with representative equipment and firefighters from all over the northeast Texas area. Mike Pell, president of the Palestine Firefighters Association, said it's the only one he knows of. You'll see all kinds of fire engines in the parade, including antiques.

November

Bloomburg
"Cullen Baker Country" Fair
First Saturday in November
Atlanta Area Chamber of Commerce, P.O. Box 29, Atlanta 75551, 903/796-3296
Admission: free

Cullen Baker deserted the Confederate Army during the Civil War and roamed the northern part of wooded Cass County committing all kinds of crimes. Fair coordinator Norene Schumann explained the festival doesn't really honor the outlaw, but that the surrounding country is often called "Cullen Baker Country," because of the man's notoriety.

The country fair features a parade, crafts display, barbecue, country store, games for children, fiddling contest and gospel music. It all takes place on the streets and sidewalks of downtown Bloomburg.

San Saba
Pecan Festival and Venison Chili Cook-off
Thanksgiving week and weekend
San Saba County Chamber of Commerce, County Courthouse, San Saba 76877, 915/372-5141
Admission: $1

San Saba is the Pecan Capital of the World as well as excellent deer hunting country. This combination festival makes for a nice autumn outing and some good eating.

Most of the pecan related events take place during the week, including judging of locally grown pecans and the Miss Pecan and Little Mr. and Miss Pecan pageants. There's also a pecan baked goods contest sponsored by the Agriculture Extension Agency.

The chili cook-off, in appreciation of deer hunters who help out the local economy with their visits, takes place in the city park Saturday. One of the organizers, W.D. Carroll, explained chili is made using the hunters' deer meat. There's also a parade, rodeo, pecan pie eating contest for kids, an arts and crafts fair, dance, and live entertainment in the park all day.

Waxahachie
A Faire on the Square
Thanksgiving weekend
Waxahachie Chamber of Commerce, P.O. Box 187, Waxahachie 75165, 903/937-2390
Admission: free; fee for homes tour

This Victorian Christmas Celebration features five historic homes decorated for Christmas, a children's bike parade, a window display contest, arts and crafts exhibits, live entertainment, and food booths representing the Victorian era.

DECEMBER

Marshall
Wonderland of Lights
Thanksgiving weekend through New Year's Day
Marshall Chamber of Commerce, P.O. Box 520, Marshall 75671, 903/935-7868
Admission: free

Marshall brightens up for the Christmas season with more than 2.5 million Christmas lights on buildings, trees, and decorations all over town. In all, the strings of light measure more than 230 miles.

Spectacular decorated scenes abound during this world-famous event, including 25 light art panels, designed and constructed by volunteers. Neighborhoods decorate with lights around a central theme.

More than 260,000 lights decorate the uptown square, covering lampposts and the courthouse museum. More than 9,000 lights bedeck a giant Christmas tree on the square. The town square is the site of various activities, including the March of the Lighted Carolers, in which 2,000 singers carry candles as they march around the square.

Each Tuesday and Thursday night, choirs, dressed in decorative robes, perform on the square. Other activities include a parade and the Jingle Bell Run. You can get driving or walking tour maps from the Wonderland Information Center on the square, open from 6 p.m. to 9 p.m. each night.

Winnsboro
Winter Trails
December
Winnsboro Chamber of Commerce, 201 W. Broadway, Winnsboro 75494, 903/342-3666
Admission: free

This is much like Winnsboro's famous Autumn Trails festival, but the focus is Christmas tree farms instead of fall foliage.

There's something happening each weekend, including crowning of the Christmas Queen and princesses, a Christmas parade, a style show, and a tour of homes. You can get maps in town that show the way to Christmas tree farms in the Winnsboro area.

★

South and Southeast Texas

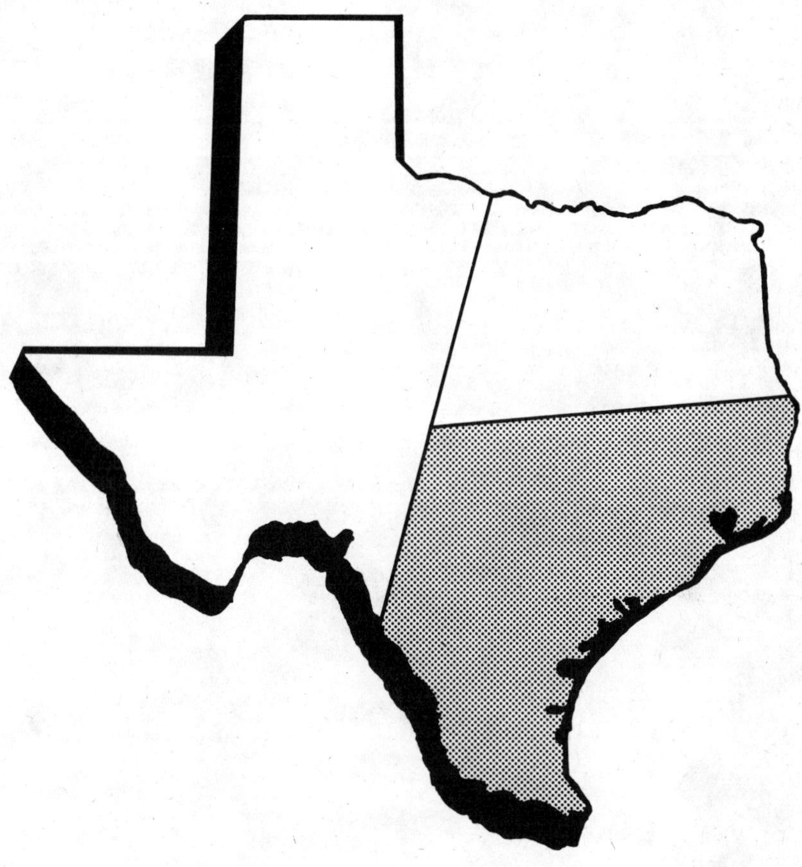

Helen Shimek of the Shimeks of Hallettsville plays the accordion for fans at the El Campo Polka Fest. *El Campo Leader-News* photo by Dawn Albright.

JANUARY

El Campo
Polka Fest
Second Sunday in January
Knights of Columbus Council 2490, Armory Road, El Campo 77437, 409/543-6557 or chamber of commerce, 409/543-2713
Admission: $5

El Campoans love to dance, and because of their rich Czech heritage, they love to polka. This music festival, sponsored by the Knights of Columbus, features a full day of music by three polka bands. Usually, at one point during the day, all the bands get on stage together for a giant jam session, and the crowd sings along to the Czech songs. Dancers from all over the state, young and old, swirl around the wooden dance floor of the KC Hall. If you don't know how to polka, this is the place to learn. There's plenty of beer, soda and food for sale.

Mission
Citrus Fiesta
Last week in January
Texas Citrus Fiesta, P.O. Box 407, Mission 78572, 512/585-9724
Admission: fees to some events

This festival, held since 1932, begins with a Fun Fair at Lion's Park, with continuous musical entertainment, citrus exhibits, children's games, craft demonstrations, food and an arts and crafts show.

Citrus Fiesta is known the world over for its Product Costume Show. Two shows feature clothing made of products grown in the Rio Grande Valley. The costumes must be completely covered with at least one kind of Valley product. This could be orange seeds, onion skins, corn husks, or any agricultural product.

The Parade of Oranges shows off area produce with a category called Valley Grown Products, in which floats must consist of at least 50 percent Valley produce. This parade attracts more than 100,000 visitors.

Other activities include a king and queen contest and plenty of contests for Winter Texans, including golf, shuffleboard and pool.

Laredo
Los Dos Laredos Winter Texan Festival
January
Laredo Chamber of Commerce, P.O. Box 790, Laredo 78042, 1-800-292-2122, 512/722-9895
Admission: free

Happy to host Winter Texans, Laredo welcomes its guests with a little party. Activities include square dancing, an arts and crafts fair, an antique car show, horseshoe tournament, a fishing contest, Mexican dance and music performances, and a model aircraft airshow.

FEBRUARY

Lovelady
Lovefest
Second Saturday in February
Houston County Chamber of Commerce, P.O. Box 307, Crockett 75835, 409/544-2359
Admission: free

Lovelady celebrates Valentine's Day with this festival, which features a parade, an arts and crafts fair, live local bands all day, and chili and barbecue cook-offs. The celebration also includes a 42 domino tournament. About 4,000 people attend this festival.

Brownsville
Charro Days Fiesta
Last Thursday in February through Sunday
Charro Days Headquarters, 612 Elizabeth, P.O. Box 1904, Brownsville 78520, 512/542-4245
Admission free to most events, but some balls cost $20 per couple

Charro Days Fiesta hearkens back to the old cowboy days of Mexico. The charro was the original cowboy, forerunner of the Western American ranch hand we know so well. Sombreros, chaps, spurs and lariats all originated on the Mexican cattle ranch.

Festivities begin officially with a grito, or yell, Thursday afternoon downtown. Costumes play a major role in Charro Days, and you'll see people in Mexican attire from various regions and time periods. You can enjoy plenty of dances and dance performances, especially various Mexican styles.

Main attractions include the Grand International Parade, the Fiesta de los Niños, which means children's festival, and the youth parade.

There's plenty of free street entertainment, including a dance. Other attractions include food booths, arts and crafts, and games.

Yoakum
Land of Leather Days
Last weekend in February
Yoakum Chamber of Commerce, P.O. Box 591, Yoakum 77995, 512/293-2309

A dog enjoys the view from a bicycle during Yoakum's Land of Leather Days. Photo by Dawn Albright.

Admission: free

The folks in the Leather Capital of the Southwest brave the unpredictable weather of February to celebrate their main industry with a chili cook-off in the charming streets of downtown Yoakum. It's just as likely to be warm and sunny as it is cold and rainy.

Fourteen companies in Yoakum make leather products, and the festival usually includes tours of one of the plants. You can shop in stores that sell leather products made in Yoakum.

The festival features the Grungiest Boot and Hat Contest, a cow chip toss, a beer can stack and a chili eating contest. There's also live music in the afternoon, a dance, a rodeo, covered wagon rides and the Rawhide Golf Tournament. You can usually watch saddlemaking demonstrations, and visit the town's historical museum, which features exhibits on the leather industry.

Edinburg
Fiesta Hidalgo
Last weekend in February
Edinburg Chamber of Commerce, P.O. Box 85, Edinburg 78540, 512/383-4974
Admission fees for rodeo, concerts and dances; the rest is free

This festival celebrates the establishment of Edinburg as the Hidalgo County seat in 1908. About 20,000 people attend each year in this Rio Grande Valley town, where February weather is usually mild.

Activities include a downtown parade, a country western dance, a food bazaar, live Tejano and rock music and a U.S. Cycling Federation- sanctioned bicycle race with a time trial and road race. There's also a carnival, a golf tournament and drag races.

Winter Texan Night features folkloric dancers, mariachi music, choir performances and a ballroom dance. Pan American University hosts plays and sporting events during the festival as well.

Laredo
Washington's Birthday Celebration
10 days in late February
Washington's Birthday Celebration Association, P.O. Box 816, Laredo 78042, 512/722-0589
Admission: fees to some events

Yes, the folks in Laredo really celebrate George Washington's birthday, and have done so since 1898. This is the nation's largest celebration in honor of our first president.

The festival features 23 events, some serious, like the black tie Colonial Ball, and some humorous and fun, like the Jalapeño Festival.

Two parades entertain visitors. The Grand National Parade consists of entries from Mexico, the United States and Texas, and lasts up to four hours. The Youth Illuminated Parade features 10,000 students from area schools whose lighted creations make a beautiful procession.

A Taste of Los Dos Laredos gives everyone a chance to sample some good food. Other activities include a sock hop, a debutante presentation and the Princess Pocahontas Western Gala. Held right after the Princess Pocahontas Debutante Presentation, the gala features debutantes wearing their Native American costumes.

There's also a 5K run, a carnival, fireworks, and charro competition. The Charreada, or Mexican-style rodeo, consists of teams performing various feats of horsemanship in a colorful presentation. The charros earn points for their skills in roping, riding, steer felling and other events, with emphasis on style rather than speed.

The Jalapeño Festival features the famous waiters' race, wherein waiters from both Texas and Mexico see who can reach the finish line first carrying a tray with a glass of champagne and an open bottle. There's also a jalapeño eating contest.

MARCH

Fulton
Fulton Oysterfest
First weekend in March
Rockport-Fulton Area Chamber of Commerce, P.O. Box 1055, Rockport 78382, 512/729-6445; in Texas: 1-800-242-0071; outside Texas: 1-800-826-6441
Admission: free

Organized by the Fulton Volunteer Fire Department, this seaside festival draws a crowd of about 50,000. Activities include an oyster eating contest, an oyster shucking contest, a kiddie carnival, a parade, an arts and crafts fair, entertainment and food booths.

Most activities take place under two large tents overlooking Aransas Bay. The parade, complete with an oriental dragon, displays the ethnic diversity of the community.

While you're there, you can belly up to the oyster bar for a plate of six. Or, sample some fried shrimp. There's live music to dance to.

Hidalgo
Borderfest
First weekend in March
Hidalgo Chamber of Commerce, 611 E. Coma, Hidalgo 78557, 512/843-2734
Admission: $4

Usually when people think of the Texas-Mexico border, they think only of the Mexican culture, said Joe Vera III, president of the Hidalgo Chamber of Commerce. Borderfest, he explained, presents the culture, crafts, food and history of the many ethnic groups in the area. These include Polish, German, Scottish, Japanese, and Korean as well as Mexican. "You really get a better understanding of their way of life," he said.

Some 25,000 people visit to sample food, listen to music and dance. Activities include the International Square Dance and Clogging Jubilee, a parade and demonstrations of crafts of various cultures.

Before the festivities begin, the officials of Hidalgo and the Mexican town of Reynosa shake hands in the middle of the international bridge. A large retinue of cloggers accompanies the Hidalgo group, while mariachi musicians walk with those from Reynosa. After greetings are exchanged, the International

Square Dance and Clogging Jubilee begins in Reynosa.

Seven stages showcase music and dancing, and a food court allows visitors to sample the diversity of South Texas cuisine. You can also see artisans demonstrate everything from pottery to blacksmithing. Other events include a carnival, a Mexican horse show, a car crushing demonstration, an antique car and truck show, and a polo match.

Washington-on-the-Brazos
Texas Independence Day
First weekend in March
Washington-on-the-Brazos State Historical Park, P.O. Box 305, Washington 77880, 409/878-2214
Admission: free

No one lives in Washington-on-the-Brazos, but it's an important place for Texans. This is where the Texas Declaration of Independence was signed March 2, 1836, while the Alamo was under siege. Six weeks later, Texas won its freedom from Mexico, beginning 10 years as an independent republic. Its days as a nation gave Texas the nickname The Lone Star State, a name that evokes pride in all true Texans.

The celebration, held in the state park and co-sponsored by the Star of the Republic Museum, of Blinn College, features historical reenactments from the era of the Republic of Texas. You'll also see historical craft demonstrations, hear fiddle and dulcimer music and witness the lighting of candles on a giant birthday cake. You get a taste it, too.

The Navasota Theatre Alliance puts on a play, and you can also see performances by cloggers, square dancers and local bands. As many as 10,000 people may attend over the two days. There's also food for sale.

Silsbee
Texas Pine Festival
Second weekend in March
Silsbee Chamber of Commerce, 835 Hwy. 96 South, Silsbee 77656, 409/385-5562 or St. Mark's Catholic Church, P.O. Box 336, Silsbee 77656, 409/385-4498
Admission: free

This started as a fundraiser for St. Mark's Catholic Church, but now involves the entire Silsbee community. They have a parade, a street dance, an arts and crafts fair, food booths, music, square dancers and a pie eating contest.

A tuba player marches in the Fulton Oyster Fest parade. Photo by Dawn Albright.

Groveton
East Texas Timber Fest
Third weekend in March
Groveton Chamber of Commerce, P.O. Box 366, Groveton 75845, 409/642-1715
Admission: $1 adults

Deep in the East Texas forests, the people of Groveton organize an event that reflects the importance of the timber industry to their community. One of the main activities is the forestry competition, in which teams of professional loggers compete in log sawing, pole felling and other lumbering skills.

They also have a chain saw demonstration and a log truck show in which trucks are judged on appearance and safety. Log haulers from all around bring their trucks for the judging and are included in the parade.

Other entertainment includes clogging, square dancing, local musicians, a dance, an arts and crafts fair, and food booths.

Liberty
Liberty Jubilee
Third weekend in March
City of Liberty, 1829 Sam Houston, Liberty 77575, 409/336-7361
Admission: free

The Jubilee starts Friday night with a fish fry sponsored by the Lion's Club and a street dance. Saturday's attractions include a parade, an arts and crafts fair, a bean cook-off, a cornbread cook-off, food booths, and a bike decorating contest. Dancers, jugglers and musicians entertain visitors. There's a musical variety show in the Humphrey Cultural Center. Texas artisans demonstrate crafts such as boatbuilding and horse shoeing.

Nederland
Nederland Heritage Festival
Third weekend in March
Nederland Heritage Festival, Box 770, Nederland 77627, contact LaDonna Floyd, secretary, at 409/727-2711

Nederland celebrates its Dutch and Cajun heritage with dancing, food, music and games. They have a parade, street dances, an indoor dance, 5K and 10K runs, a skateboarding competition, a bicycle race, and pageants. If you're looking for ethnic food, the Dutch groups sell ice cream and cookies, and the Cajuns sell gumbo, boudin and rice balls.

You might want to check out the Windmill Museum, built to preserve the town's Dutch heritage. Exhibits and artifacts relate Nederland's history.

Hallettsville
South Texas Polka and Sausage Fest
Third weekend in March
Knights of Columbus Hall, P.O. Box 46, Hallettsville 77964, 512/798-2311
Admission: $5 per day per person

Saturday night's dance contest attracts polka and waltz experts from around the state. On Sunday, three bands keep dancers moving around the floor of the large Hallettsville Knights of Columbus Hall.

Not only will you find sausage, but also sauerkraut, German potatoes, homemade chicken noodle soup and kolaches to eat.

Newton
Wild Azalea Spring Festival
Last weekend in March or first weekend in April
Newton County Chamber of Commerce, P.O. Box 66, Newton 75966, 409/379-5527
Admission: free

This celebration of one of nature's most beautiful gifts takes place as far east as you can go in Texas. Wild azaleas grow between steep forested hills, blooming pink in the early spring.

A pocket of wilderness near Newton shelters a large concentration of wild azaleas and longleaf pine amid rock cliffs. Temple-Eastex Inc., the lumber company that owns the land, maintains nature trails open only during the azalea bloom season. At the canyons, you'll find hospitality tables and guided tours.

Back in town, the Newton Garden Club puts on its annual flower show. You'll also find live entertainment, square dancing, music by local bands, a stagecoach on display, and food booths.

Bridge City
Texas Crawfish and Saltwater Crab Festival
Last full weekend in March
Bridge City Chamber of Commerce, 150 W. Roundbunch,

Bridge City 77611, 409/735-7671 or Betty Hogg, chairwoman, Crawfish Festival Committee, Route 11, Box 142, Orange 77630, 409/745-1242
Admission: $1 adult

Rice and crawfish being major products of Southeast Texas, Bridge City folks know how to cook and eat them both. Eating contests feature prominently in this festival, with a crawfish eating contest for the public and one for members of the news media. There are also crawfish races for both groups. While all this is going on there's Cajun music all day, played by well-known performers.

You can stroll through the arts and crafts fair and eat food galore, mostly crawfish dishes. Douget's Rice of Beaumont donates rice to the festival each year, much of which is given away in drawings held every 30 minutes. They give away other prizes besides rice, too. For kids, there's a carnival.

Woodville
Dogwood Festival
Last weekend in March and first weekend in April
Tyler County Chamber of Commerce, 201 N. Magnolia, Woodville 75979, 409/283-2632
Admission: free

Since 1940, they've been celebrating the smooth white flowers of the dogwood, one of the first trees to bloom in spring. The blossoms seem to float in the leafless understory of the forest when the nights are still cool. If you've never seen dogwood blossoms, you must go to East Texas in early spring.

Woodville's festival includes a parade, a dance, contests, a trail ride, arts and crafts, live entertainment, and food booths.

★

APRIL

Marble Falls, Burnet, Lake Travis, Llano, Buchanan Dam, Kingsland and Lampasas
Highland Lakes Bluebonnet Trail
Late March and early April
Highland Lakes Tourist Association, P.O. Box 1967, Austin 78767, 512/478-9085
Admission: free; fees for some activities

The Bluebonnet, the official state flower of Texas, blooms in late March and early April. Several towns in the Hill Country along the Colorado River, where bluebonnets grow in abundance, have festivals and arts and crafts fairs during the flowering period.

Burnet
Burnet Bluebonnet Festival
Second weekend in April, usually
Burnet Chamber of Commerce, P.O. Drawer M, Burnet 78611, 512/756-4297

Burnet's salute to the state flower features a parade, dances, arts and crafts, food booths, 5K and 10K runs and a 25-mile bike race through the countryside. There's also a bluebonnet and wildflower arrangemant contest and a flower photography contest. Other entertainment includes the Fort Hood Army Band and other live music, snake handlers, a domino tournament, a fly-in at the airport, a carnival and a beauty pageant.

Kingsland
Bluebonnet Festival
First weekend in April
Kingsland/Lake LBJ Chamber of Commerce, P.O. Box 465, Kingsland 78639, 915/388-6211

Kingsland's activities include a 10K volksmarch, bluebonnet trails, bicycle tour, bicycle rodeo, music, children's games, chili cook-off, horseshoe pitching, arts and crafts, washer pitching contest, martial arts exhibition and barbecue dinner.

Llano
Highland Lakes Bluebonnet Trail
Second and Third weekends in April
Llano Chamber of Commerce, 700 Bessemer, Llano 78643,

915/247-5354

Llano has been celebrating the bluebonnet spring show for 25 years. Besides bluebonnet tours, Llano has an old time fiddler's contest, food booths and an arts and crafts fair.

Lampasas
Bluebonnet Fair
First Saturday in April
Lampasas County Chamber of Commerce, PO Box 627, Lampasas 76550, 512/556-5172
Admission: free

The Bluebonnet Fair features a fish fry, antique car show, live music, food booths, a bike and tricycle decorating contest, and an arts and crafts fair.

Alvin
Rice and Crawfest
First Saturday in April
Alvin-Manvel Area Chamber of Commerce, P.O. Box 2028, Alvin 77512, 713/585-8662
Admission: free

The low, flat, easy-to-flood land of Alvin is ideal for both rice and crawfish farming. The festival includes a gumbo cook-off, an arts and crafts exhibit, a crawfish dinner, and live music. You'll also find children's games, dancing, horseshoe pitching, a dunking booth, and food booths.

Bay City
Heritage Day
First Saturday in April
Bay City Chamber of Commerce, P.O. Box 768, Bay City 77414, 409/245-8333
Admission: free

Bay City greets spring with activities at the town square and old railroad depot. They have a mini-parade, historic crafts demonstrations, food booths, and live entertainment all day.

Demonstrations include butter churning, flint knapping, weaving, and washing clothes in a tub. You'll find music, square dancers, cloggers, and ballet. Also a pie-eating contest, carriage rides, a wildflower exhibit, and kids games.

Harlingen
Riofest
First or second weekend in April

Harlingen Chamber of Commerce, P.O. Box 189, Harlingen 78551, 512/423-5440
Admission: $2

Riofest celebrates the arts and the ethnic diversity of Harlingen's community on the border with Mexico.

Arts and crafts, music and food abound in this event. You'll see all kinds of arts and crafts demonstrations, and hear a variety of ethnic music representing all types of Texans — German, Mexican, Scottish and others.

Held in Harlingen's Fair Park, the festival features several craft and entertainment areas. You may also hear lectures on various topics ranging from bird rescue to Mayan culture, and attend workshops in such folk arts as pottery, basketweaving and silk screening. There's a kid's area with games, face painting and the works.

Other events include a chili cook-off, a bicycle race and 5K and 10K fun runs.

Round Top/Winedale
Winedale Spring Festival and Texas Crafts Exhibition
First weekend in April
Winedale Historical Center, Box 11, Round Top 78954, 409/278-3530
Admission: $2 adult; 50 cents students

Some of Texas' leading contemporary artists show their work at Winedale in a juried crafts show. You'll find woodworkers, potters, basketweavers, jewelrymakers, metal-workers and others, all in the quiet, green setting of Winedale's restored pioneer building complex.

While touring the buildings, you can watch demonstrations of crafts such as spinning and weaving, soapmaking, fireplace cooking, corn shucking and rawhide chair making.

Other events include a German play, hands-on pottery demonstrations, dinner, and music performances. There's a dance, folk, jazz and classical music performances, and an outdoor dinner.

While you're in the area, you could visit nearby Round Top, where the Square Fair and Antique Fair are going on.

Poteet
Poteet Strawberry Festival
Second weekend in April (depends on Easter)
Poteet Strawberry Festival Association, Box 227, Poteet 78065, 512/742-8144

Admission: yes; covers all activities except food

A short drive south from San Antonio lies the Strawberry Capital of Texas — Poteet. Its annual festival attracts 90,000 visitors to sample the luscious crop. Activities include a parade, a dance, strawberry judging and auction, a fiddler's contest, an arts and crafts fair, a rodeo and a carnival.

Six large stages feature continuous entertainment, including music, ethnic dancing and clowns. Food booths sell strawberry ice cream, Poteet Strawberry Festival Wine, strawberry cheesecake, strawberry shortcake and strawberry parfait.

Bellville
Country Livin' Festival
Second weekend in April
Bellville Chamber of Commerce, P.O. Box 670, Bellville 77418, 409/865-3407
Admission: free

Bellville attracts about 13,000 people with this spring festival, which includes a dance, self-guided bluebonnet trails, antique show, craft demonstrations and horseshoe tournament. There's also a hayride, an arts and crafts fair, tours of county jail museum, Little Mr. and Miss Bluebonnet pageant, a biergarten, a stage show, and food booths.

Freer
Rattlesnake Round-Up
Mid-April
Freer Chamber of Commerce, P.O. Box 717, Freer 78537, 512/394-6891
Admission: $2 adults

This began in 1965 as the Freer Oil-O-Rama with oilfield equipment displays, airshow and beauty pageant. Back in those days, oilfield crews often met face to face with rattlesnakes, which made their work dangerous, not to mention unpleasant. So they began having snake-catching contests during Oil-O-Rama. Eventually the snake hunting became so popular it dominated the festival and inspired the new name.

Now, the Rattlesnake Round-up features a parade, daredevil snake shows with live cobras and rattlesnakes, a dance, contests, an arts and crafts fair, live entertainment, rodeo, the Miss Freer pageant, and food booths.

Portland
Portland Pioneer Days

Mid-April (depends on Easter)
Portland Chamber of Commerce, P.O. Box 388, Portland 78374, 512/643-2475
Admission: free

Pioneer Days hosts a crowd of about 25,000 people who come for the parade, outdoor music, a street dance, games, arts and crafts, and food booths. There's also a fajita cook-off, a style show, a pageant, a golf tournament, a carnival, and an auction.

Smithville
Smithville Jamboree
Weekend after Easter
Smithville Chamber of Commerce, P.O. Box 716, Smithville 78957, 512/237-2313
Admission: $5 for adults; includes dances

The Jamboree features two downtown parades, dances at night, an arts and crafts fair, a fireworks display, and horseshoe and washer pitch tournaments. They usually have a day when senior citizens get free admission.

The festivities take place at Crockett River Bend Park on the Colorado River just outside Smithville. There's plenty of food for sale, so bring your folding chair and enjoy.

Beaumont
Neches River Festival
Week after Easter
Beaumont Convention and Visitors Bureau, P.O. Box 3827, Beaumont 77704, 409/880-3749, 1-800-392-4401
Admission: free

This festival celebrates both the Neches River and the school students of Beaumont, with many activities centering around educational accomplishments.

The second weekend of the festival is probably the best for visitors with its downtown parade, boat show and chili cook-off. You'll also find a costume contest, a bicycle race, a flower show, a flotilla, and an arts and crafts show. There's plenty of music and other entertainment. Many festival activities are at the city's Riverfront Park.

Burton
Cotton Gin Festival
Third weekend in April
Operation Restoration, Inc., P.O. Box 132, Burton 77835, 409/

289-5102
Admission: $2 adult

The Burton Farmer's Gin is one of the few remaining complete cotton gin and mill complexes in the United States. That is, it contains cotton gin technology from the beginning of ginning up to 1974. Plans are in the works to make the gin a national museum, in cooperation with the Smithsonian Institution.

The festival raises money for restoration of the buildings, as well as celebrating Burton's heritage. There's plenty of live entertainment both Saturday and Sunday, including contemporary and country and western bands, folk music and vocalists.

Other activities include a parade, a fireworks display, a sausage cook-off, ice cream and pie eating contests, farm equipment displays, an arts and crafts fair, food booths, and a carnival.

Dripping Springs
Founders Day and Chicken Cook-off
Third weekend in April
Dripping Springs Founders Day, P.O. Box 578, Dripping Springs 78620, 512/858-4740
Admission: free

This celebration includes a parade, a chicken cook-off, a street dance, arts and crafts, contests, live music, a fiddler's contest, horseshoe and washer pitch contests, and a car show.

Huntsville
General Sam Houston Folklife Festival
Third weekend in April
Huntsville Chamber of Commerce, P.O. Box 538, Huntsville 77342, 1-800-289-0389
Admission: $5 adult

Dozens of civic groups in the Huntsville area work together to honor General Sam Houston, the first president of the Republic of Texas, and to celebrate the state's folklife heritage.

The festival takes place on the grounds of the Sam Houston Memorial Museum, where Houston built his home, and in Pritchett Field, on the campus of Sam Houston State University, next to the museum grounds.

As many as 16,000 people may attend over three days. The festival showcases different parts of Texas' ethnic culture, including Indian, German, Hispanic, Irish, African-American,

An Indian dancer performs during the General Sam Houston Folklife Festival in Huntsville. Photo courtesy General Sam Houston Folklife Festival.

Polish, Scottish and others. In each area, you can sample ethnic food, hear music, and observe folk art demonstrations.

You'll experience a variety of other entertainment on the wooded grounds of the museum, including music, storytellers, dancing, singing and dramatic performances. You may see people dressed as historic figures who knew Houston. You can visit the museum, see Sam Houston's home and eat plenty of good food.

Mauriceville
Crawfish Festival
Third weekend in April
Crawfish Festival Committee, Sybil Jenkins, P.O. Box 683, Mauriceville, 77626, 409/745-3777
Admission: $2 adult

Crawfish farming is a new industry in Texas, started in the early 1980s. Of course, people in Southeast Texas have been eating crawfish Cajun-style for a long time.

The Crawfish Festival includes a parade, a dance, a crawfish eating contest, a crawfish cooking contest, a crawfish calling contest, an arts and crafts fair, and music.

Somerville
Spring Festival
Third weekend in April
Somerville Chamber of Commerce, P.O. Box 352, Somerville 77879, 409/596-2383
Admission: $2 per car entrance fee to state park

The boat parade visible from Welch Park at Lake Somerville makes this festival unique. Decorated boats of all shapes and sizes plow the waves between the mainland and an island. There's also a dance at night, a variety of games, food booths, horseshoe pitching, a chili cook-off, an arts and crafts fair, live entertainment, and bingo.

Kirbyville
Magnolia Festival
Third weekend in April
Kirbyville Chamber of Commerce, P.O. Box 417, Kirbyville 75956, 409/423-5827
Admission: free

The tallest Pyramid Magnolia in the United States grows near Kirbyville, at the edge of Newton County. In Texas, this small version of magnolia grows naturally only in Newton and Jasper counties, in the eastern part of the Big Thicket.

This tree on private property has a circumference of 76 inches, a height of 57 feet and a crown spread of 37 feet, said Ron Dosser of the Texas Forest Service.

The largest Southern Magnolia in Texas is in the next county, just outside of Jasper. This giant tree has a trunk circumference of 194 inches, is 112 feet tall, and has a 45 foot crown. It grows on property owned by the Louisiana-Pacific Timber Co.

The festival honoring this tree with the fragrant flowers features a parade, a dance, contests, an arts and crafts fair, live entertainment, a pancake breakfast, a 5K run and walk, food booths, and a carnival.

West Columbia
San Jacinto Festival
Third weekend in April
West Columbia Chamber of Commerce, P.O. Box 837, West Columbia 77486, 409/345-3921
Admission: free

This festival pays tribute to the Texan victory over the Mexican Army at San Jacinto in 1836, when Texas won its independence from Mexico. West Columbia became the first official capital of the Republic of Texas and the meeting place of the Columbia Congress, which elected Sam Houston president and signed the constitution.

The festival includes historical tours, the Belle of the Brazos pageant, a volleyball tournament, helicopter rides, a parade, a dance, contests, arts and crafts, entertainment, and food booths.

Montgomery
Trek and Trades
Third week in April
West Montgomery County Chamber of Commerce, P.O. Box 1, Montgomery 77356, 409/597-4155
Admission: free, except for homes tour

They've been holding the Trek, a tour of historic homes, since 1954 in Montgomery. The Trades part of the festival includes a parade, an arts and crafts fair, food booths, country cooking, and a variety of entertainment.

Snook
Snookfest

Third Saturday in April
Snookfest, P.O. Box 10, Snook 77878, call City Hall at 409/272-3021
Admission: free

Snookfest features a parade at 10 a.m., antique farm equipment exhibits, an arts and crafts fair, games, and horseshoe, washer, and domino tournaments.

You can hear Czech and country music in the park all day while you sample some of the Mexican, Czech and other foods for sale. A children's barnyard and an evening dance at the fire station complete the schedule.

Crystal Beach
Texas Crab Festival
Last weekend in April
Bolivar Peninsula Chamber of Commerce, P.O. Box 1170, Crystal Beach 77650, 409/684-5940
Admission: small parking fee

Bring a folding chair to this beach festival, where you can see a crab cook-off and a sandcastle building contest. They also have crab races, the crab legs contest, live entertainment by area bands, food booths, arts and crafts, carnival rides, seafood and a variety of beach games.

Hallettsville
Texas State Championship Fiddler's Frolics
Fourth weekend in April
Hallettsville Chamber of Commerce, P.O. Box 313, Hallettsville 77964, 512/798-2662 or Knights of Columbus Hall, 798-2311
Admission: $5

This weekend musical celebration started in 1970. The fun includes two nights of live bands, usually country and Cajun. You can hear good fiddle music all weekend, played by musicians of all shapes and sizes. There's also dancing, arts and crafts, food booths, a fun run, and a barbecue cook-off. The fiddling competition takes place Saturday. On Sunday, they choose the champion fiddler and induct players into the Texas Fiddler's Hall of Fame.

La Porte
Sylvan Beach Festival
Last Saturday in April
La Porte-Bayshore Chamber of Commerce, P.O. Box 996, La

Contestants warm up backstage for the Texas State Championship Fiddler's Frolics in Hallettsville. Photo by Dawn Albright.

Porte 77572-0996, 713/471-1123
Admission: $1 adult

Since 1956, La Porte has celebrated its seashore, Sylvan Beach, with this festival that draws about 25,000 people. Events include a parade, dance, live entertainment, music, a chili cook-off and a variety of games. There's also a Miss Sylvan Beach contest.

★

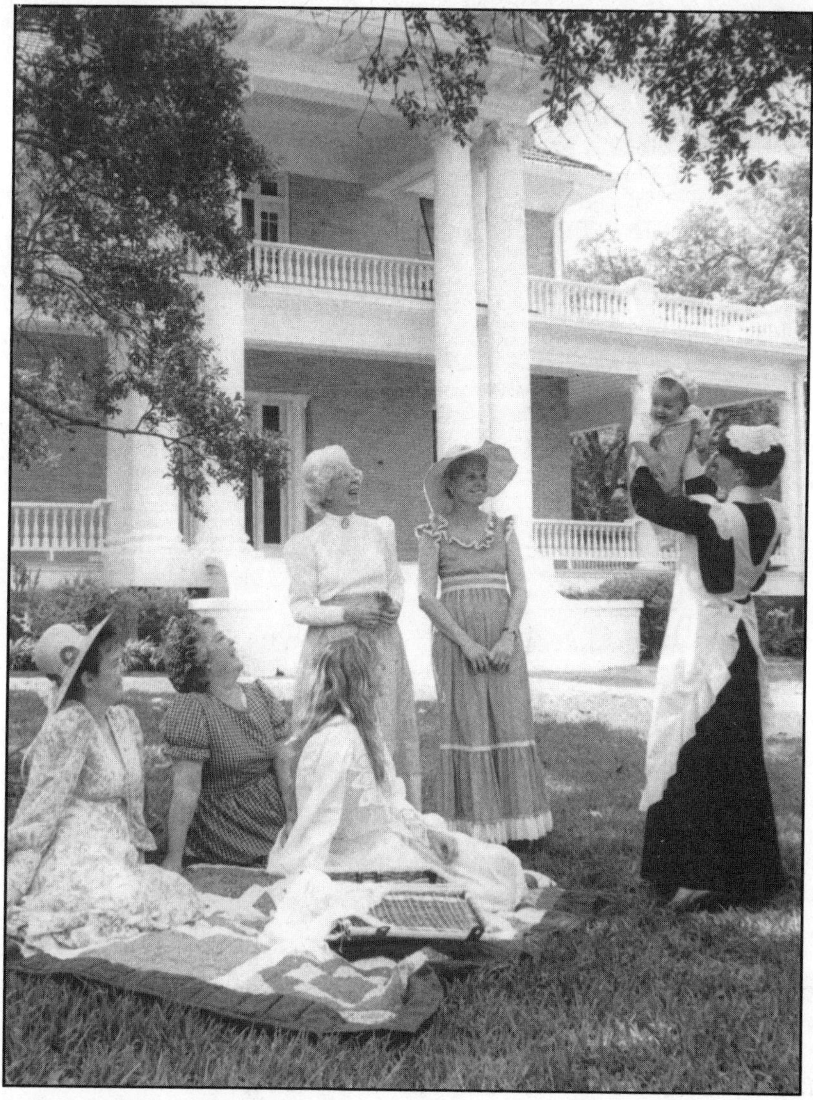

Participants dress in old-fashioned clothing during Navasota Nostalgia Days. Photo courtesy the *Navasota Examiner*.

MAY

Ingleside
Round Up Days
May
Ingleside Chamber of Commerce, P.O. Box 686, Ingleside 78362, 512/776-2906
Admission: free

Ingleside, on the edge of Corpus Christi Bay, holds a parade, a dance, a bike-a-thon, a bean cook-off, and a horseshoe tournament. There's also an arts and crafts fair, beauty pageant, carnival, talent show, and music.

Falfurrias
Fiesta Ranchera
First weekend in May
Falfurrias Chamber of Commerce, P.O. Box 476, Falfurrias 78355, 512/325-3333
Admission: free

This festival features a western dance, a trail ride, arts and crafts, entertainment, and food booths. There's also a carnival, a rodeo, live music and games.

Navasota
Nostalgia Days
First weekend in May
Grimes County Chamber of Commerce, P.O. Box 530, Navasota 77868, 409/825-6600
Admission: free

You can step back to the turn of the century in Navasota during Nostalgia Days, when townspeople dress in clothing typical of that period. Well-restored Victorian buildings provide a rich backdrop for this event, which features a parade, a street dance, live music, and home tours.

Among the types of music you may hear are Dixieland jazz, western swing and folk. There's plenty of entertainment by cloggers, square dancers and others.

Activities include a juried arts and crafts show, hay rides, a carnival, a quilt show and theatre performance.

Orange
International Gumbo Cook-off
First weekend in May

Greater Orange Area Chamber of Commerce, 1012 W. Green Ave., Orange 77630, 409/883-3536
Admission: free

This event, paying tribute to that spicy, delicious Cajun stew we call gumbo, has three tent dances featuring Cajun, Zydeco and country and western music. You'll also find a parade, plenty of food, arts and crafts, a children's area, storytelling, a fun run, and plenty of other entertainment. It all takes place in downtown Orange.

Rosenberg-Richmond
Fort Bend Czechfest
First full weekend in May
Rosenberg-Richmond Chamber of Commerce, 4120 Ave. H, Rosenberg 77471, 713/342-5464
Admission: $4

Music, dancing, food, and crafts give visitors a thorough view of Czech culture in Texas. You'll see people in traditional Czech festival costume, Czech imports, and Czech dance performances. The event also offers a kolache bake-off, children's games and a carnival.

Alice
Fiesta Bandana City Celebration
Ten days surrounding May 5
Alice Chamber of Commerce, P.O. Box 1609, Alice 78333, 512/664-3454
Admission: free

To celebrate Cinco de Mayo, the people of Alice put on a 10-day event with special activities on May 5. Alice Mayor and schoolteacher Octavio Figueroa works with children to produce a play about Cinco de Mayo, the Mexican holiday observing the Battle of Puebla. On May 5, 1862, Mexican soldiers defeated an invasion of French troops south of Mexico City.

The big day includes the play, ballet folklorico, mariachi music, food booths and arts and crafts. During the rest of the festival, there's entertainment every night, including an area-wide talent show, a prince and princess contest, a beautiful baby contest, and a 5K run.

Beaumont
Beaumont Cinco de Mayo Festival at Riverfront Park
Weekend closest to May 5

Beaumont Convention and Visitors Bureau, P.O. Box 3827, Beaumont 77704, 409/880-3749, 1-800-392-4401
Admission: free

Beaumont's remembrance of the Battle of Puebla includes a parade, a queen's pageant, a jalapeño eating contest, a piñata party, arts and crafts, and plenty of Mexican food. You'll be entertained by mariachis and folk dancers.

Goliad
Cinco de Mayo Festival
Saturday closest to May 5
Goliad Chamber of Commerce, P.O. Box 606, Goliad 77963, 512/645-3563
Admission: free

Goliad has a special connection with May 5, the date of the Battle of Puebla, since the Mexican general in the battle, Ignacio Zaragosa, was from Goliad. Mexico wasn't a strong country back then; in fact, the French invaded because Mexico owed them money. Zaragosa led a ragtag army into battle with the French and won.

Attractions include a dance, an arts and crafts fair, ballet folklorico, Miss Zaragoza Coronation, a commemorative mass, appearances by international dignitiaries, and food booths.

Beaumont
Kaleidoscope Creative Arts Festival
Mother's Day weekend
Beaumont Convention and Visitors Bureau, P.O. Box 3827, Beaumont 77704, 409/880-3749, 1-800-392-4401
Admission: $2.50 adult, $2 senior citizen

Kaleidoscope features juried artists and artisans showing their work, and continuous live music including jazz, bluegrass and barbershop quartets. Other entertainment includes poetry readings, ballet, and performances by cloggers, square dancers, jugglers and storytellers.

You'll find plenty of food. There's also an "art alive" area where craftspersons demonstrate their skills in glass blowing, sketching, pottery and other arts.

This is sponsored by the Art Museum of Southeast Texas, and takes place in downtown Beaumont on 5-acre grounds.

Brenham
Maifest
Thursday, Friday, Saturday before Mother's Day

Washington County Chamber of Commerce, 314 South Austin, Brenham 77833, 409/836-3695
Admission: $4

Brenham's Maifest grew out of a traditional German festival started in the 1880s. Now, Brenham folks celebrate their children and their German heritage with this large and lively event.

The children's parade kicks off the festival Friday, with kids up to junior high school age dressed in all sorts of costumes from starfish to rose petals. Saturday, the high school seniors get the spotlight with their parade.

There's German music in the beer garden Friday night, and Saturday and Sunday from noon till midnight. If you don't polka, you can still enjoy watching others fly around the dance floor.

"There's a lot of German heritage here, and the old-timers get out there on the dance floor and show the younger ones how it's done," said Melani Bayless of the Washington County Chamber of Commerce.

Other attractions include a variety of games, a carnival, coronations of kings and queens, food booths featuring German and other foods, and an arts and crafts fair.

The Blue Bell Ice Cream factory offers free tours Monday through Friday. Saturday there are no tours, but the visitors center is open.

Weimar
Weimar Gedenke Country Fun Festival
Saturday before Mother's Day
Weimar Chamber of Commerce, P.O. Box 90, Weimar 78962, 409/725-8675
Admission: free

Gedenke means "remember" in German, and the folks in Weimar recall their history with this street festival. They organize a parade, a street dance, live music during the day, an arts and crafts fair, and food booths selling everything from homemade ice cream to famous Weimar sausage. There's also a Miss Weimar contest and a fun run.

Columbus
Magnolia Homes Tour and Live Oak Arts and Crafts Show
Third weekend in May
Columbus Chamber of Commerce, P.O. Box 343, Columbus 78934, 409/732-5881

Admission: free

During this festival of Columbus' heritage, girls stroll the sidewalks in antebellum gowns and surreys roll through streets shaded by giant oak trees. Events include an arts and crafts fair, an auction, family night on the square, surrey rides, live entertainment, performances in the opera house, and a beer garden.

Pflugerville
Deutschen Fest
Third weekend in May
Pflugerville Chamber of Commerce, P.O. Box 483, Pflugerville 78660, call City of Pflugerville, 512/251-3076
Admission: $2 adult; purchase of t-shirt gets free admission

This festival glorifying Pflugerville's German heritage features a parade, an outdoor dance, arts and crafts, a fun run, games, music and other entertainment, plus plenty of food for sale.

Among the entertainment, you'll hear folk singers, blues and other music. They have activities for kids, such as a balloon man and magician.

Jourdanton
Jourdanton Days Kactus Kick
Third weekend in May
Jourdanton Chamber of Commerce, P.O. Box 747, Jourdanton 78026; contact Dorothy Manning at 512/769-3087 or chamber at 512/769-2158
Admission: free; fee for dance

This festival used to be called Dairy Days, back when dairy farms thrived in the area. Now, The Kactus Kick includes a chili cook-off, a parade, dances on Friday and Saturday nights, a trail ride, arts and crafts fair, Miss Jourdanton Pageant, food booths, and a 10K run. Live entertainment Saturday afternoon usually includes dancers representing various ethnic groups.

People in Jourdantan love to get silly, so they have the No Talent Show on Friday night, and the Anything Goes Contest Saturday afternoon. In the No Talent Show, participants get points for their lack of performance ability, as long as it's entertaining, explained Dorothy Manning, an organizer of the event.

The Anything Goes Contest challenges the adventurous with hilarious tasks involving eggs, obstacle courses, tires, wheel barrows, and water balloons.

Vidor
Texas Bar-B-Q Festival
Third weekend in May
Vidor Chamber of Commerce, P.O. Box 413, Vidor 77662, 409/769-6339
Admission: free

This event features a barbecue cook-off, a car show, a parade, a dance, an arts and crafts fair, food booths, a horseshoe pitching contest, a queen contest, and a tiny tot pageant.

Bandera
Funteir Day
Memorial Day weekend Saturday
Bandera County Chamber of Commerce, P.O. Box 171, Bandera 78003, 512/796-3045
Admission: free

This festival in the Cowboy Capital of the World commences with a parade in the morning, then continues with live entertainment all day. There's a trail ride, contests, arts and crafts fair, dances and food booths.

Kerrville
Kerrville Folk Festival
Last weekend in May and first two weekends in June, Thursday through Monday
Kerrville Folk Festival, P.O. Box 1466, Kerrville, 78029, 512/257-3600
Admission: $6 to $12 one day; discounts available

The Kerrville Folk Festival features new and established folk musicians and groups playing in an outdoor amphitheatre in the Texas Hill Country. The peaceful, easygoing, family atmosphere of this music event makes it one people return to year after year.

During the day, you'll find a special children's stage, arts and crafts for sale, and people playing music everywhere.

Main entertainment begins in the evening, with about six artists performing each night. You may sit on benches, bring your own folding chair, or spread a blanket on the ground. Food for sale at the amphitheatre includes plate lunches and dinners, including something for vegetarians.

Camping is available at the Quiet Valley Ranch, where the festival is held. It's a great place to bring your children, as there's children's entertainment. You may notice the line at the smoothie booth is longer than the line at the beer booth.

Although the Kerrville Folk Festival is operated for profit, it's listed here because it's unique.

Kerrville
Texas State Arts and Crafts Fair
Memorial Day weekend Friday through Sunday
Texas State Arts and Crafts Fair, P.O. Box 1527, Kerrville 78029, 512/896-5711
Admission: $6 one day for adults, $3.50 one day for children; excellent discounts and family rates available

If you want to buy fine arts and crafts, this is the place to shop. Spread over the hilly fairgrounds at Kerrville's Schreiner College, the fair showcases more than 200 of Texas' best artists and craftspeople. You'll find everything from pottery to furniture.

This family-oriented event also offers music, food, a laser light show, old-fashioned games, and demonstrations of historic skills and crafts. Each year, demonstrators choose two historic crafts to show in detail, in addition to all the others. You may see soapmaking, lacemaking, furniture making, or weaving.

Killeen
Festival of Flags and Rodeo
Memorial Day weekend
Greater Killeen Chamber of Commerce, P.O. Box 548, Killeen 76540, 817/526-9551
Admission: free

Celebrating the variety of their cultural heritage, the people of Killeen put on a colorful festival that attracts about 7,000.

Festivities include a parade Saturday morning, a street dance Saturday night, and in between, plenty of arts and crafts, international foods for sale and ethnic music. There's a Volksmarch, a PRCA rodeo, a barbecue cook-off, a cobbler cook-off, and a Mexican hat dance. The antique car show includes a period costume contest.

Port Lavaca
Texas Summerfest
Memorial Day weekend
Port Lavaca-Calhoun County Chamber of Commerce, P.O. Box 528, Port Lavaca 77979, 512/552-2959
Admission: free except for dances

Summerfest has two dances, one on Friday and one on

Saturday night. Other activities include games, an arts and crafts fair, a fishing tournament, food booths, live entertainment, a carnival, and the Miss Summerfest pageant.

Presidio
Onion Festival
Last part of May
Presidio Chamber of Commerce, P.O. Box 1405, Presidio 79845, 915/229-3199

Presidio, the Onion Capital of the World, celebrates for three days with menudo and onion cook-offs, recognition of the best farmer and best citizen, and onion farm tours. An award goes to the person who grows the largest onion. A parade, a dance, an arts and crafts fair, the Onion Queen contest, and food booths complete the attractions.

Round Rock
Fiesta Amistad
Memorial Day Weekend
Round Rock Chamber of Commerce, 212 E. Main, Round Rock 78664, 512/255-5805
Admission: $4 adult

Fiesta Amistad offers visitors a parade, a dance, live entertainment, music and food. The Round Rockers usually showcase some well known Hispanic musicians, as well as country and western bands. Contests include tamale eating, tortilla spreading and beer drinking.

JUNE

Mason
Pinto Bean Cook-off
June
Mason County Chamber of Commerce, P.O. Box 156, Mason 76856, 915/347-5758
Admission: free

Celebrities from radio, television and the literary world judge the creations of the pinto bean cooks. Besides the cook-off, there's a dance, contests and food booths.

Yoakum
Yoakum Leather Tom Tom Festival
First Saturday in June
Yoakum Chamber of Commerce, P.O. Box 591, Yoakum 77995, 512/293-2309
Admission: free

The Tom Tom Festival started in 1928 when Yoakum was a tomato growing and shipping center. In 1973, the organizers added leather to the name in honor of the town's newer major industry. Fourteen companies in Yoakum make leather products, ranging from saddles to belts and wallets.

Contests in honor of the tomato include bobbing for tomatoes, a tomato relay, tomato toss, tomato recipe cook-off, and prize tomato judging.

During the festival, the Yoakum Heritage Museum opens its leather room, which features original hand tooling and old and new leather products. A parade through Yoakum's brick-building downtown highlights the celebration. Other attractions include three dances (two during the week), a rodeo, a barbecue cook-off, an 8K fun run, arts and crafts, and live music all day Saturday.

Contests include marshmallow eating, jalapeño eating, men's sexy legs, women's sexy legs, toilet paper unrolling, kite flying and an old fiddler's competition. There's also a beauty pageant, quilt show, carnival, and rodeo queen contest.

Madisonville
Madisonville Sidewalk Cattlemen's Association Celebration
First week in June
Madison County Chamber of Commerce, 118 S. Elm, Madisonville 77846, 409/348-3591

Admission: $3; includes sampling of barbecue cook-off entries

The Sidewalk Cattlemen's Association regulates the wearing of cowboy boots in Madison County. That is, if you don't own any cattle, you're not supposed to wear boots.

In 1941 Henry B. Fox, publisher of the *Madisonville Meteor*, wrote a column making fun of people who wore cowboy boots but owned no cattle. The next week, he announced (jokingly, of course), in his column that the Madisonville Sidewalk Cattlemen's Association (MSCA) had been formed. The Associated Press put this information on its wire, and people all over the country read about the boot wearing regulations of Madison County.

A girl in Boston read about it, and happened to be looking for a pair of cowboy boots to wear in her school play. So little Audrey Mangan wrote a letter to the MSCA, which the local post office sent to the *Meteor*. Fox showed it to some of his friends, and they decided to have a barbecue and invite the girl. So they flew her down from Boston, and that was the beginning of the Celebration.

Now, many years later, they have a parade, dance, trail ride, barbecue cook-off, arts and crafts, music and rodeos.

Pearsall
Pearsall Potato Festival
First weekend in June
Pearsall Chamber of Commerce, 317 S. Oak, Pearsall 78061, 512/334-2242
Admission: $2 adult

Pearsall has the only potato festival in Texas, held to mark the end of the potato harvest. Events include a potato cook-off and auction, as well as other games and contests relating to the potato. There's also a parade, dance, live entertainment and food booths.

Blanco
Blanco Valley Jamboree and Fiddlefest
Second weekend in June
Blanco Chamber of Commerce, P.O. Box 626, Blanco 78606, 512/833-5101
Admission: free

This festival began as a fiddler's contest, so the festivities revolve around music. Besides old time fiddling, you can see performances by Hill Country musicians and cloggers. Other entertainment includes a parade, dance, arts and crafts fair, 5K and 1K races, and usually a chili, barbecue or bean cook-off. There are plenty of games for both kids and grown-ups at this community get together with attendance of about 1,000.

Crockett
World Champion Fiddler's Festival
Second weekend in June
Houston County Chamber of Commerce, P.O. Box 307, Crockett 75835, 409/544-2359
Admission: $3 adult

Fiddlers perform in an open-air pavilion not far from historic downtown Crockett. A Friday night dance gets things going. Other attractions include arts and crafts, clogging performances, and plenty of food for sale, much of it homemade like pies and sausage.

Lockhart
Chisolm Trail Round-up
Second weekend in June
Lockhart Chamber of Commerce, P.O. Box 840, Lockhart 78644, 512/398-2818
Admission: free except for dances and rodeo

Chisolm Trail Roundup features a full-blown festival combined with the Lockhart Kiwanis Club Rodeo. The four-day event features dances every night, a children's and regular parade, barbecue and chili cook-offs, a 5K run, an old time fiddler's contest, a carnival, and food booths.

The re-enactment of the Battle of Plum Creek dramatizes one of the last major battles between settlers and Indians.

Boerne
Berges Fest
Father's Day Weekend
Boerne Area Chamber of Commerce, 1 Main Plaza, Boerne 78006, 512/249-8000
Admission: free

Berges means "hills" in German. So the folks in Boerne, in the Hill Country along the Guadalupe River, celebrate the beauty of the countryside with this event. A parade, a dance, contests, pig races, canoe races, horse races and a bike rally are some of the featured events. There's also an arts and crafts fair, food booths, and free entertainment under the pavilion.

Brenham
Washington County Juneteenth Celebration
Father's Day weekend or weekend closest to June 19
Washington County Juneteenth Association, P.O. Box 1505, Brenham 77833, 409/836-1097
Admission: $2 to $4

June 19 marks the anniversary of the end of slavery in Texas. Although the Civil War ended April 9, 1865, people in Texas didn't stop fighting for two months, and did not hear about the Emancipation Proclamation until June 19. On that day, U.S. Gen. Gordon Granger read the proclamation in Galveston and gave orders to free the slaves. The day became an official state holiday in 1979.

The folks in Washington County start the festivities Friday night with the coronation of royalty for the parade. On Saturday morning the parade moves through Brenham's beautifully restored historic downtown. For an hour before the parade begins, a blues band on the courthouse square entertains spectators.

After that, most activities take place at the Washington County Fairgrounds. Attractions include music by various blues and contemporary bands, a dance, food booths, and a variety of games. There's usually a trail ride and carnival as well.

Garwood
Rice Festival
Father's Day weekend
Garwood Community Association, P.O. Box 198, Garwood 77442, 409/758-9085
Admission: free; small fee for rice tasting

The highlight of this event in this rice farming community is the rice tasting, wherein visitors may sample dishes entered in the rice cooking contest. Festival organizer Mary Till said as many as 75 expert rice gourmets enter the competition. For the price of a ticket, visitors may eat all the rice they want.

Other attractions include craft booths, food booths, a carnival, chili and barbecue cook-offs, a dance, turtle races, antique booths, an antique tractor show and live entertainment on an outdoor stage. It all takes place on Garwood's main street, just off Highway 71.

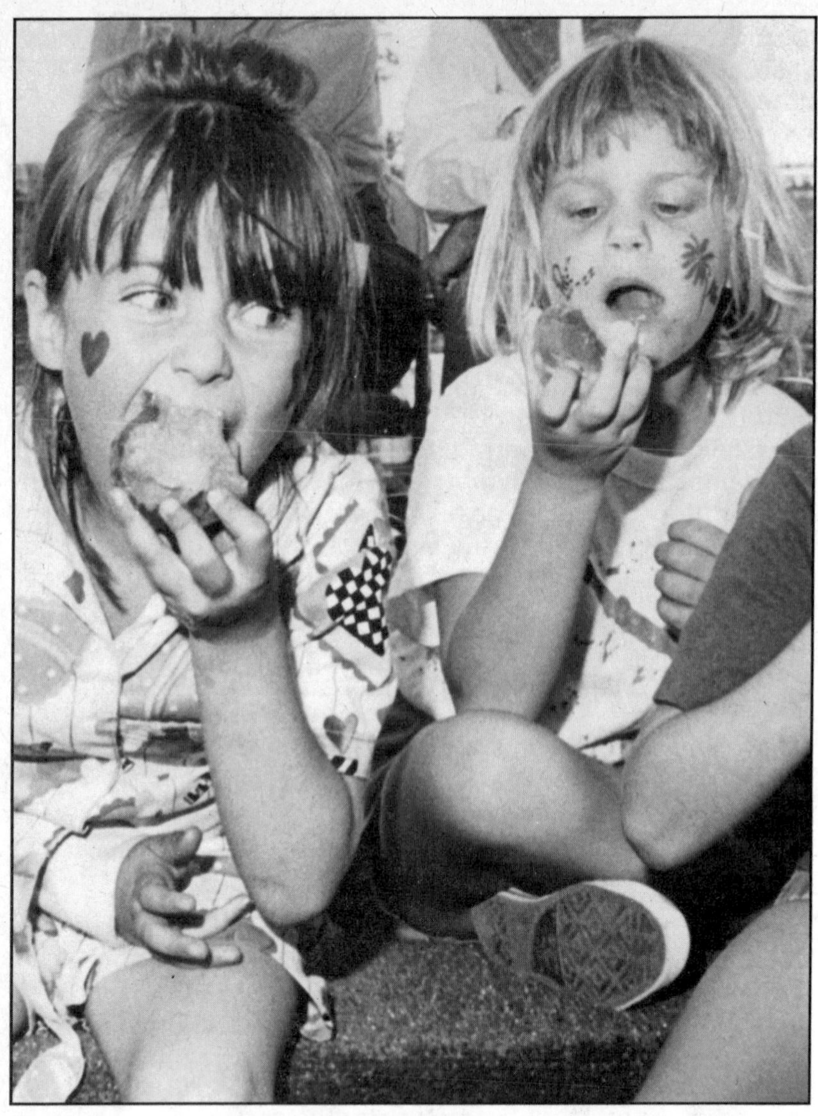

Young girls gobble peaches during the Stonewall Peach JAMboree. Photo courtesy *Fredericksburg Standard-Radio Post.*

Stonewall
Stonewall Peach JAMboree
Third weekend in June
Fredericksburg Chamber of Commerce, P.O. Box 506, Fredericksburg 78624, 512/997-6523
Admission: $4 adult

Stonewall's peaches are famous all over Texas, and this is a great chance to taste the fruit and get in on the fun of celebrating it.

The festival includes a parade, peach pie and cobbler baking contest, peach eating contest, pit spitting contest, continuous entertainment, a rodeo, and a peach auction. The Peach Patch children's area features a petting zoo, clowns, face painting and storytelling. There's plenty of food for sale, from barbecue to peaches and ice cream.

Sabinal
Cypress City Celebration
Third weekend in June
Sabinal Chamber of Commerce, P.O. Box 55, Sabinal 78914, 512/988-2010
Admission: free

The town of Sabinal and the Sabinal River were both named for the Cypress trees that grow there. Sabinal is Spanish for Cypress.

Since 1964, the people have honored this natural heritage with various events including a dance, contests, arts and crafts, stage show, food booths, rodeo and sports tournaments.

Goliad
Longhorn Stampede
Third Friday and Saturday in June
Goliad County Chamber of Commerce, P.O. Box 606, Goliad 77963, 512/645-3563
Admission: free

In 1976, to celebrate the U.S. Bicentennial, folks in Goliad organized a "stampede" of 100 longhorn cattle through downtown Goliad, calling it the "fastest parade in history."

They had so much fun that day they decided to honor the occasion each year. The festival now features a dance on Friday and Saturday nights, an arts and crafts fair, food booths and heritage arts demonstrations like blacksmithing. Live entertainment includes Indian dancers, cloggers, storytellers and puppets.

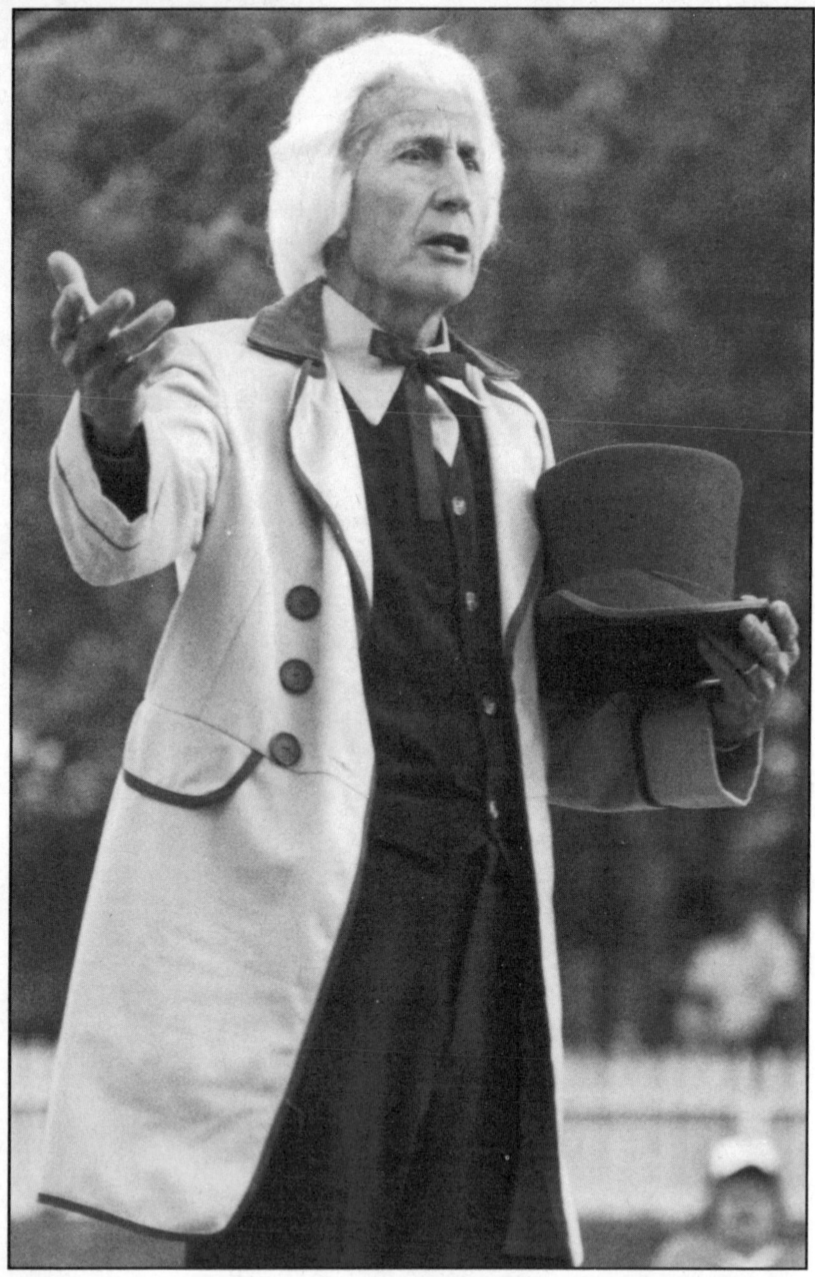

A volunteer portrays a character from the early days of Texas during the General Sam Houston Folklife Festival in Huntsville. Photo courtesy General Sam Houston Folklife Festival.

Although there's no longer a stampede, you can see longhorns and even get your picture taken sitting on one. A popular event (and effective fundraiser) is the Longhorn Plop. This is also known as cow chip bingo, in which players purchase a square drawn on the ground in a roped off area. A few well-fed longhorns are set loose in the corral, and the crowd watches to see where the cattle will "plop."

Stockdale
Stockdale Watermelon Jubilee
Third weekend in June
Stockdale Chamber of Commerce, P.O. Box 366, Stockdale 78160, contact Patty Stahl, secretary-treasurer, 512/996-3866
Admission: free except for dance and rodeo

This fruit festival started in 1945, and now features a parade, two dances, a rodeo, a queen coronation, a cow chip toss, children's games, arts and crafts, and food booths. The Watermelon Olympics includes watermelon eating and seed spitting contests.

Texas City/LaMarque
Mainland Funfest
Third weekend in June
Texas City-LaMarque Chamber of Commerce, P.O. Box 3330, Texas City 77592, 409/935-1408
Admission: free

Funfest features a parade, a country and western dance, a two-day arts and crafts fair, a bicycle ride and fun run, games, an antique car show and a barbecue cook-off. You'll also find carnival rides, kite flying and windsurfing.

Luling
Luling Watermelon Thump
Last Thursday, Friday and Saturday in June
Luling Watermelon Thump Association, P.O. Box 710, Luling 78648, 512/875-3214
Admission: free; fees for dances

The Guinness World Record for watermelon seed-spitting is held by Lee Wheelis of Luling, who spat a seed 68 feet, 9 1/8 inches during the 1989 Thump.

He broke a previous record set by John Wilkinson of Austin, who shot a seed 65 feet, 4 inches from his mouth at Luling in 1980.

About 35,000 people visit Luling, a major watermelon shipping site, for the Thump. Activities include a parade, three street dances, a team seed-spitting contest, rodeo, carnival, arts and crafts, and food booths.

Watermelon events include watermelon eating contests, champion melon auction, and championship seed spit-off.

Florence
Florence Friendship Days
Fourth weekend in June
Florence Chamber of Commerce, P.O. Box 507, Florence 76527, call Union State Bank, 817/793-2601
Admission: free

This festival in northwest Williamson County, with an attendance of about 3,000, is held on Florence's main street. It features a parade, street dance, arts and crafts fair, 5K run, music, variety of games and plenty of food.

JULY

Belton
Belton's Independence Day Celebration and PRCA Rodeo
Week of July 4
Belton Area Chamber of Commerce, P.O. Box 659, Belton 76513, 817/939-3551
Admission: free except for rodeo

Belton began celebrating Independence Day in 1850. July 4 features a parade, patriotic program, gospel singing, country and western music, dance and an old fiddler's contest. There's also an arts and crafts fair, food booths, carnival and games for children. The professional rodeo usually runs for three days before or after July 4.

Goliad
Celebration of American Cultures
July 4
Goliad State Park, P.O. Box 727, Goliad 77963, 512/645-3405
Admission: $2 per car entry to state park

This showcases Texas culture with music, dancing and crafts demonstrations. The crafts include weaving, pottery, flintknapping, natural dying and bowmaking. Mariachis, Indian dancers, folksingers and gospel choirs entertain visitors. The event is held in Goliad State Historical Park-Mission Espiritu Santo Compound.

Weesatche
Weesatche Fourth of July Festival
July 4
Goliad Chamber of Commerce, P.O. Box 606, Goliad 77963, 512/645-3563
Admission: free

This fire department fundraiser started in 1960. Festivities include a dance, contests, arts and crafts, food booths, family style barbecue, a general store with homemade canned and baked goods and quilt raffles.

Kingsland
Kingsland Aqua Boom
July 4 weekend
Kingsland/Lake LBJ Chamber of Commerce, P.O. Box 465, Kingsland 78639, 915/388-6211

Admission: free except for pageant and dance

This summer festival features water and land parades, dances, a music festival, barbecue, arts and crafts, food booths, fireworks on the 4th, a water ski show and a jet ski show.

Palacios

Lion's Club Fourth of July Celebration

July 3 & 4

Palacios Chamber of Commerce, P.O. Box 774, Palacios 77465, 512/972-2615

Admission: free except for dance

The shore of Palacios Bay teems with people during this festival, held since 1950. Activities include a parachute jump demonstration, live entertainment, food booths, bingo, a carnival, kiddie rides, and a fireworks display. An evening dance takes place in a pavilion built over the water.

Seguin

Freedom Fiesta

July 4 weekend

Seguin-Guadalupe County Chamber of Commerce, P.O. Box 710, Seguin 78155, 512/379-6382

Admission: free

The Seguin July 4 event has a parade, dance, game booths for kids, food booths, cloggers, old time music bands, and a dance and firweorks in the evening. They also have all-girl and old-timers rodeo.

Round Rock

Frontier Days and Old Settler's Reunion

Weekend after July 4

Round Rock Chamber of Commerce, 212 E. Main, Round Rock 78664, 512/255-5805

Admission: fees for some activities

Frontier Days offers visitors a parade, street dance, arts and crafts, 5K run, games, music and food. You can see children's ballet folklorico and reenactments of the legendary Sam Bass shootout, which took place at Round Rock.

Other activities include square dancers, washer pitch and horseshoe contests, a puppet show, a cannon shootout, fence painting, a chicken flying contest, watermelon seed-spitting and pepper eating.

Victoria
International Armadillo Confab and Exposition
July 7 - generally, but not necessarily
International Armadillo Appreciation Society, P.O. Box 2465, Victoria 77902, 512/573-5277
Admission: free

Major events include armadillo races and the Miss Vacant Lot of the World and Surrounding Counties Extravaganza. This is a parody of beauty contests everywhere, and any woman over age eight may enter.

Henry Wolff, a columnist for the *Victoria Advocate,* said of the Miss Vacant Lot contest, "It's more or less a spoof on beauty contests in general."

The number of contestants ranges "anywhere's from one to 40. I think the first year they had one," Wolff said.

"They can do anything, or not do anything. Talent is helpful but not required. It's mainly left to the eye of the judges, who can generally be bought. The winner gets a trophy and almost certain obscurity."

One popular event is the hop, skip and jump parade around DeLeon Plaza. There are no motorized floats — everyone's on foot. Trophies are awarded for the best parade entries.

Besides this silly stuff, you'll also find armadillo races, music all day and most of the night, arts and crafts, local folk musicians, food booths and whatever else may occur. Proceeds from all this benefit the Boys and Girls Club of Victoria.

Santa Fe
Annual Crab Festival
Third weekend in July
Santa Fe Chamber of Commerce, P.O. Box 681, Santa Fe 77510, 409/925-8558 or Veterans of Foreign Wars Post #5400 and Auxiliary, 409/925-9971
Admission: free

Organized by the VFW Post and Auxiliary, this festival celebrates the delicious shellfish. Activities include a free outdoor dance Friday night and an indoor Cajun dance Saturday night. They have crab races, barbecue, pork and gumbo cook-offs, a horseshoe tournament, an arts and crafts exhibit and food booths.

Shiner
Shiner Half-moon Holidays
First weekend in July

Mimes dance in the street during Victoria's International Armadillo Confab and Exposition. Photo by Richard Goldsmith.

Shiner Chamber of Commerce, P.O. Box 221, Shiner 77984, 512/594-4180
Admission: free

Shiner remembers its original name with this summer festival. David Kaspar, a festival organizer, explains the original settlement was about a half-mile from where it is now, near a grove of trees shaped like a half-moon, called Half-moon Timber. So the town was called Half-moon.

In the late 1800s, the railroad came close to Half-moon, but not close enough. Since everyone wanted to be near the railroad, they moved, naming the new settlement after Henry B. Shiner, who donated a piece of land for the town.

The festival starts with a dance on Saturday night and continues Sunday with a parade, 10K run, chili cook-off, arts and crafts fair, and food booths. The Half-moon Olympics includes picnic games like tug-of-war, 3-legged races and sack races. There's also a Miss Shiner pageant, noon meal, and auction.

Shiner is famous for the Spoetzl Brewery, which makes Shiner Premium beer and Shiner Bock, that dark brew beloved of beer drinkers all over Texas. The brewery began in 1909 when German and Czech citizens formed the Shiner Brewing Association to satisfy their longing for Old World-style beer. Kosmos Spoetzl, a Bavarian beermaker, bought the brewery in 1914 and began making his recipe, which they've used ever since.

Spoetzl prides itself on having the smallest commercial brewing kettle in the United States — 75 barrels — and on performing most brewing tasks by hand.

Although it's not open on the weekends, you can tour the plant Monday through Thursday at 11 a.m. and visit the Hospitality Room for a taste of Shiner Monday through Friday.

Elgin
Elgin Western Days
Fourth weekend in July
Elgin Chamber of Commerce, P.O. Box 408, Elgin 78621, 512/285-4515
Admission: free

Elginites organize a parade, street dance, rodeo, arts and crafts fair, carnival, horseshoe toss, tug of war and arm wrestling. Other competitions include cooking and needlework. There's also plenty of food and beer available.

Clute
Great Texas Mosquito Festival
Last weekend in July
Brazosport Chamber of Commerce, 420 Hwy 332, Clute 77531, 409/265-2505
Admission: free

The much-disdained but ever-present mosquito is the honoree of this lowland festival. Some of the most interesting events are the mosquito song writing competition, mosquito legs look alike contest and the mosquito calling contest. There's also a Mosquito Juice Chug-a-lug, Ms. Quito pageant, and 5K and one-mile Mosquito Chase races.

Besides the mosquito events, you'll find a dance, arts and crafts fair, fajita cook-off, chili cook-off, haystack dive, live bands, beautiful baby competition and food booths. The festival, held at Clute Municipal Park, draws a crowd of about 20,000.

Medina
Texas International Apple Festival
Last Saturday in July
Medina Development Corporation, P.O. Box 125, Medina 78055, 512/589-7224
Admission: small fee

Apples are new on the Texas farming scene, but apple growers are promoting their industry with gusto. Medina, in sparsely populated Bandera County, is known as the Apple Capital of Texas. This hilly area gave birth to the apple industry in Texas, explained Roy Goodwin, operations manager for Love Creek Ranch, a leading apple producer.

As cattle ranching became less profitable, Texans looked for other ways to make money in agriculture. Hill Country folks started growing apples in about 1980, and began selling them in 1987 as the trees matured. Now, 15 varieties grow well in the Texas Hill Country, some developed especially for the area, Goodwin said.

Most Apple Festival activities take place in a pecan grove, so there's plenty of shade. Festivities include a dance, an arts and crafts show, and a variety of food, including apple delights of all kinds. You can taste apple cider, apple ice cream, apple sauce, apple butter, strudel, syrup and baked apple goods. There's an apple pie contest, judging of the local crop and apple bobbing.

Local growers sell their fruit and its products. The Try-apple-on challenges competitors in several races involving apples. You can tour an apple orchard in a double-decker bus.

Live music all day, including a fiddler's contest, provides a festive atmosphere. Black powder rifle shooting, an archery contest, mule rides and a volksmarch round out the events.

AUGUST

Winedale
Shakespeare at Winedale Festival
Three weekends in August
Shakespeare at Winedale, P.O. Box 11, Round Top, 78954, 409/278-3530
Admission: no fee to enter grounds; $3 to see play

Since 1970, students from the University of Texas at Austin have spent six summer weeks learning Shakespeare's plays, then performing them in a barn-like open-air theatre in the rolling hills of South Central Texas.

Even if you've never read or seen a play by Shakespeare or anyone else, you must experience Winedale. The students are not drama majors, but come from different departments of the university to earn credit for an English class and have lots of fun.

The atmosphere is casual (sometimes quite warm, as well, so fans are provided), with the audience sitting on folding chairs close to the actors.

You had better call ahead for reservations. Each Saturday, they serve Winedale Hunter's Stew for $5 a plate at 5 p.m. You can also see the buildings of the Winedale Historical Center, from the era of German settlement of Texas. There's a nature trail nearby, and you can always picnic on the grounds.

Schulenberg
Schulenberg Festival and German/Czech Fest
First full weekend in August
Schulenberg Chamber of Commerce, P.O. Box 65, Schulenberg 78956, 409/743-3023
Admission: $3 to German/Czech Fest

Schulenberg Festival features a parade, dance, trail ride, arts and crafts exhibits, a stage show, food booths, a carnival, team roping, a chili cook-off and a fun run.

The Schulenberg German/Czech Fest takes place Saturday. It starts at 2 p.m. in the air-conditioned American Legion Hall in Wolter's Park, with live music and dancing all day. You can partake of German and Czech food, such as sausage, sauerkraut, kolaches, beer, wine coolers and soda pop.

Hitchcock
Hitchcock Good Ole Days
Third weekend in August
Hitchcock Chamber of Commerce, P.O. Box 389, Hitchcock 77563, 409/986-9224
Admission: free

The folks in Hitchcock honor their past and have a good time together with a parade, a dance, contests, an arts and crafts fair, stage show, food booths, and a carnival.

Pleasanton
Cowboy Homecoming
Third weekend in August
Pleasanton Chamber of Commerce, P.O. Box 153, Pleasanton 78064, 512/569-2163
Admission: $1; also entry fee to rodeo

Pleasanton, in the area where ranching as we know it developed, calls itself the "Birthplace of the Cowboy." This festival honors area working cowboys.

The late Ben Parker, founder of the Cowboy Homecoming and a local community leader, researched the subject and found that Pleasanton lies within an area where raising cattle on horseback began, said Chris Troell, news editor of the *Pleasanton Express*.

"He was one of those fellows who was a visionary. He was a dreamer and also a doer," Troell said of the Pleasanton legend. She described him as a colorful character known for his playful exaggerations in storytelling.

Parker and his wife started the Longhorn Museum, with exhibits and artifacts relating to ranching and Atascosa County history.

According to Parker's research, Spanish missions in South Texas began raising cattle in 1690. At that time, they harvested the cattle with guns and bow and arrow. Eventually, individuals got into cattle raising, which led to the practice of branding, to mark their private property. They worked out a system using ropes and corrals to catch and hold the cows for branding. This marked the beginning of ranching as we know it, and the birth of the cowboy.

The festival includes a parade, dance, contests, trail ride, arts and crafts, stage show, food booths, domino tournament, 10K run and, a chili cook-off.

Castroville
St. Louis Day Celebration
Sunday closest to August 25
Castroville Chamber of Commerce, P.O. Box 572, Castroville 78009, 512/538-3142
Admission: free

The original Castroville settlers came from the Alsace province in France, famous for being much fought-over by France and Germany. With a land grant from the Republic of Texas, Henri Castro brought the Alsatians over in 1844. They brought their culture, cuisine and unwritten language, founding what is now known as the "Little Alsace of Texas," the only Alsatian community in the United States.

The settlers built their houses from limestone and cypress abundant in the area. Many of these still stand, well-preserved and listed in the National Register of Historic Places.

This festival, sponsored by St. Louis Catholic Church, began in 1882 as a parish picnic and now attracts 10,000 people. It celebrates the birthdate of the patron saint of the parish, Louis IV of France.

The day begins with a mass in historic St. Louis Catholic Church. Afterward, everyone heads for the picnic of barbecue and Alsatian sausage. There's also an auction, bingo, kiddie rides, performances by the Flemish and Alsatian Dancers of Texas, games and arts and crafts.

Besides the picnic, there's plenty of other food for sale, including an Alsatian specialty called parisa, made with raw ground sirloin. It all culminates with a dance in the evening.

Georgetown
Fiesta Georgetown
Fourth weekend in August
Georgetown Chamber of Commerce, P.O. Box 346, Georgetown 78627, 512/863-4546 David Lira, Hispanic Business Association, 512/869-4626
Admission: free except for some music performances

Sponsored by the Hispanic Business Association, the proceeds of Fiesta Georgetown go into a scholarship fund for minority students.

Fiesta Georgetown features a dance, contests, arts and crafts exhibit, food booths and an antique and classic car show. Contests include a tamale eating contest, jalapeño eating contest, menudo cook-off and guacamole mixing.

SEPTEMBER

Santa Fe
Cockroach Festival
September
Santa Fe Chamber of Commerce, P.O. Box 681, Santa Fe 77510, 409/925-8558 or Fraternal Order of Eagles 409/925-3668
Admission: free

Like Clute's Great Texas Mosquito Festival, this event recognizes another pesky insect, the omnipresent cockroach, which grows large and daring in South Texas.

The highlight of the Cockroach Festival is the cockroach race. Nita Smith, president of the Ladies Auxiliary of the Fraternal Order of Eagles, which started the event, explained the bugs race in a box with 10 lanes. When the gate opens, race officials bang the back of the cage, sending the roaches scurrying to the finish line. There's prize money for the fastest roach and the largest roach.

"Those little ones run pretty fast," Smith said. Her own entry one year, Sewer Sam, didn't even budge when the starting clang sounded. "I must have fed him too much," she said.

Besides the roach competition, there's a barbecue cook-off with prize money. A dance starts things off Friday night. Saturday features a parade, live entertainment, usually including the Rosharon Prison Choir, food, and arts and crafts booths.

Belton
Ye Olde Trade Days
Labor Day weekend
Belton Area Chamber of Commerce, P.O. Box 659, Belton 76513, 817/939-3551
Admission: free

Ye Olde Trade Days features a barbecue cook-off, carriage rides, an antique car show, a dance, arts and crafts, entertainment by local musicians, square dancing, old time music, and food booths.

Bertram
Oatmeal Festival
Labor Day Weekend
Burnet Chamber of Commerce, P.O. Drawer M, Burnet 78611, 512/756-4297
Admission: free

The Oatmeal Festival started in 1978 as a protest to the virtually empty town of Oatmeal being removed from the official state map. The town is back on the map now, but the festival proved so popular, the people involved still hold it every year.

The action begins Friday evening with a fun run followed by a supper in the community center. Saturday features a parade, oatmeal cook-off, oatmeal box stacking contest, the World Championship Oatmeal Eating Contest, and the children's Grasshopper Parade, in which kids enter pet bugs.

You'll also find a barbecue lunch, food booths, a flea market, live music, square dancers, cloggers and a street dance.

Nixon
Nixon Feather Fest
Labor Day Saturday
Nixon Chamber of Commerce, P.O. Box 56, Nixon 78140, 512/582-1977
Admission: free except for dances

Nixon celebrates its poultry industry with this festival, highlighted by a chicken cook-off. Contest categories include fried, barbecued and exotic. Other activities include a parade, street dance, arts and crafts fair, 5K run, and games for kids and grown-ups.

Rockport
Fiesta en la Playa
Labor Day Weekend
Rockport-Fulton Area Chamber of Commerce, P.O. Box 1055, Rockport 78382, 512/729-6445; toll-free in Texas, 1-800-242-0071; outside Texas, 1-800-826-6441
Admission: free

This fun beach event includes live music, a tamale eating contest, a piñata contest, kiddie carnival, macho legs contest, ballet folklorico performances, and food booths.

Brady
World Championship Barbecue Goat Cook-off and Arts and Crafts Fair
Saturday of Labor Day weekend
Brady Chamber of Commerce, 101 E. First, Brady 76825, 915/597-2420
Admission: free

Festivities start Friday night with a free dance. Saturday entertainment in Richards Park on Brady Creek includes an arts and crafts fair, fiddling, western bands, a goat pill flip-off, a blindman's wheelbarrow race, a tobacco spittin' contest, horseshoe pitching, and children's games. Of course, the cook-off itself provides plenty of laughs, with many cooks competing for showmanship awards. Saturday ends with a street dance on the courthouse square.

Anahuac
Texas Gatorfest
Opening weekend of alligator season, usually first or second weekend in September
Anahuac Area Chamber of Commerce, P.O. Box R, Anahuac 77514, 409/267-4190
Admission: $2 adult

Anahuac celebrates its role as the Alligator Capital of Texas with a parade, two dances, games and food. Anahuac earned this title because in Chambers County, alligators outnumber people.

Attractions include horseshoe pitching, arts and crafts, gator chunkin (a contest involving throwing plastic alligators), two stages of entertainment, a gumbo cook-off, food booths, an alligator education tent, an antique car display, kiddie rides and games, and The Great Texas Alligator Round-up. You can get a look at Big Al, a 13 1/2-foot alligator.

Caldwell
Kolache Festival
Second Saturday in September
Caldwell Chamber of Commerce, P.O. Box 126, Caldwell 77836, 409/567-7979
Admission: free

About 15,000 people attend this festival honoring that delicious Czech pastry known as the Kolache. Kolache actually means "little bread" in Czech. But when you add some apricot or pineapple, "little bread" takes on a whole new meaning.

There's a parade, a dance, folk dancing and music, contests, arts and crafts, a large quilt show, food booths, an antique auto and engine show, a mini-museum, Czech movies, Kolache baking competition, and a model railroad exhibition.

Port Aransas
Port Aransas Days
Second weekend in September
Port Aransas Chamber of Commerce, P.O. Box 356, Port Aransas 78373; in Texas: 1-800-242-3084; outside Texas: 1-800-221-9198
Admission: free

This celebration by the sea includes a parade, a street dance, contests, an arts and crafts fair, local talent on stage, food booths, and a gumbo cook-off. There's also a scenic dinner cruise. Port Aransas is a great place to visit. All you need to look fashionable on the island is an old T-shirt, loose shorts and flip flops.

Aransas Pass
Shrimporee
Third weekend in September
Aransas Pass Chamber of Commerce, 452 Cleveland, Aransas Pass 78336, 512/758-3713 or 1-800-633-3028
Admission: $1

Aransas Pass is known as the Shrimp Capital of the World, and since 1948, the folks there have been boasting on that with the Shrimporee. They organize a parade, a shrimp eating contest, arts and crafts, food booths, an outhouse race, a sexy legs contest, and a children's area. Most activities take place in Roosevelt Stadium.

Giddings
Geburtstag (Birthday of Giddings)

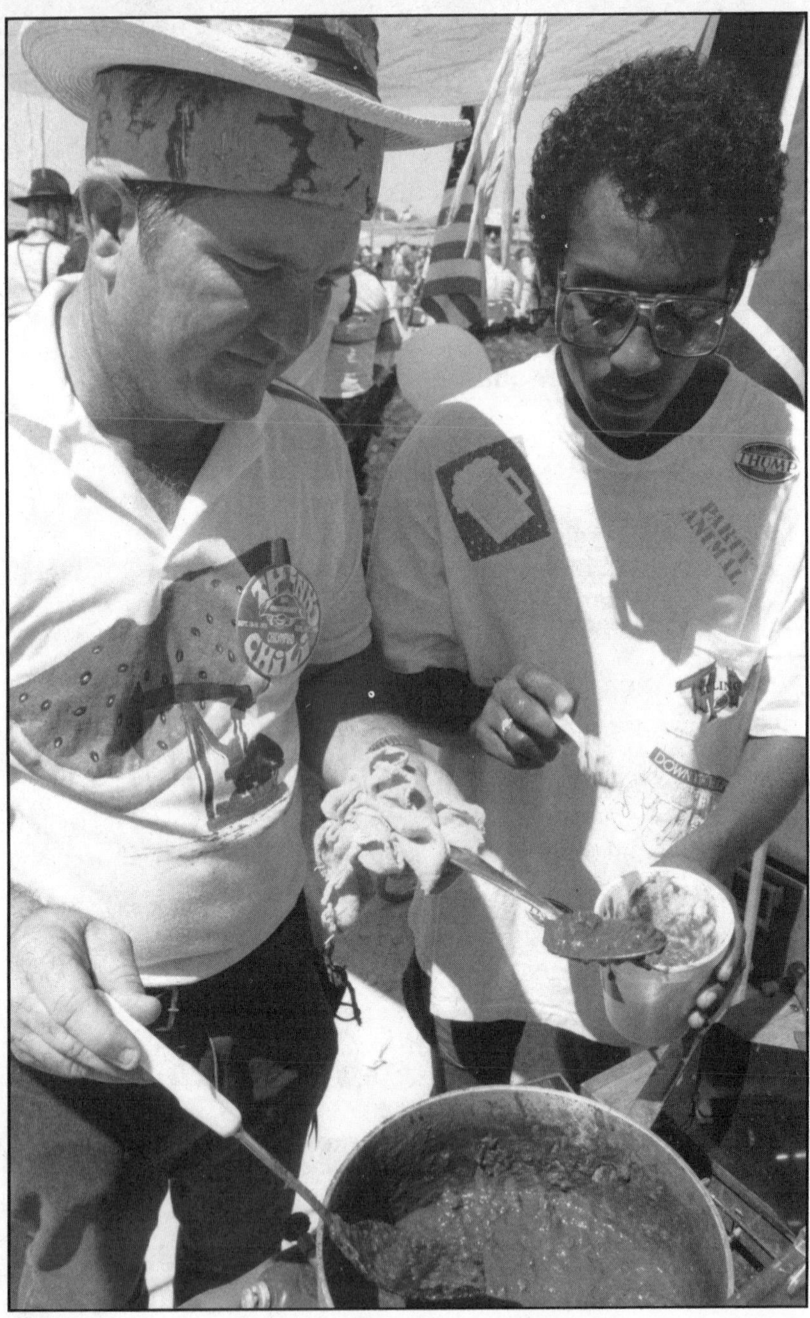

Chili lovers scoop it up at the Republic of Texas Chilympiad in San Marcos. Photo courtesy Texas Department of Commerce.

Third Saturday in September
Giddings Chamber of Commerce, P.O. Box 180, Giddings 78942, 409/542-3455
Admission: $2 adult

The folks in Giddings have been celebrating their town's birthday since 1969. The community's official beginning was in 1871. They organize a parade, a dance, arts and crafts, food booths, the Miss Giddings and Little Mr. and Miss Giddings contests, a pet show, and hobby horse rides for children. Contests include arm wrestling, washer pitching, horseshoe pitching, and a barbecue cook-off. There's live music, including German singers, all day in the park.

Karnes City
Town and Country Days
Third weekend in September
Karnes City Chamber of Commerce, 314 E. Calvert, Karnes City 78118, 512/780-3112
Admission: free

Festival activities center around the railroad and the Crazy Red Horse Saloon, a renovated cotton gin owned by the Town and Country Days Association. During the festival, this historic building serves as a beer saloon.

Events include a parade, a dance, contests, an arts and crafts exhibit, a stage show, food booths, old time crafts demonstrations, an antique engine show, a carnival, and a petting zoo.

Beeville
Diez y Seis
Weekend closest to September 16
Fiesta Bee County Inc., 110 N. Washington, Beeville 78102, 512/358-4900 or Bee County Chamber of Commerce, P.O. Box 4099, Beeville 78104, 512/358-3267
Admission: $2 adult

This features three nights of musical entertainment, including Tejano, conjunto, and country and western. Saturday night there's an alcohol-free teen dance separate from the adult dance. Besides all the great music, you'll find a chili cook-off, a menudo cook-off, pan de campo bake-off, ballet folklorico, Miss Diez y Seis pageant, a carnival, food booths, and an arts and crafts fair.

Proceeds from this non-profit event go to scholarships for the pageant winners, and to other community organizations. It's all held on the grounds of the Bee County Coliseum.

San Marcos
Republic of Texas Chilympiad
Third weekend in September
Republic of Texas Chilympiad, P.O. Box 188, San Marcos 78667, 512/396-5400
Admission: $1 to $5

Chilympiad, the men's state championship chili cook-off, determines which men get to compete at the World Championship Chili Cook-off at Terlingua in November. More than 500 entrants cook up pots of the spicy stew for the judges. The women's state championship chili cook-off takes place the first weekend in October in Luckenbach.

Held on the grounds of the Hays County Civic Center, Chilympiad includes dances, a parade, 5K run, concerts and dance performances.

West Columbia
Republic Days
Third weekend in September
West Columbia Chamber of Commerce, P.O. Box 837, West Columbia 77486, 409/345-3921
Admission: $5 covers all three days

West Columbia celebrates Texas' days as an independent nation with this event. West Columbia was the first official capital of the Republic of Texas, and the site of the first Congress.

Festivities start Friday night with five bands playing bluegrass music. Saturday you can watch people practicing skills used by pioneers in the days of the Republic right next to a replica of the First Congress building.

Crafts include spinning and weaving, soapmaking, and blacksmithing. Other attractions include a dance, contests, an antique show, food booths, and more bluegrass music, so bring a lawn chair and have a good time.

You'll also find storytellers, and a reenactment of an army camp set up by the Brazoria Militia. For a separate fee, you can tour five historic buildings in East Columbia.

Gonzales
Come And Take it Days
Weekend closest to October 2
Gonzales Chamber of Commerce and Agriculture, P.O. Box 134, Gonzales 78629, 512/672-6532

This attracts about 25,000 people to Gonzales' two large

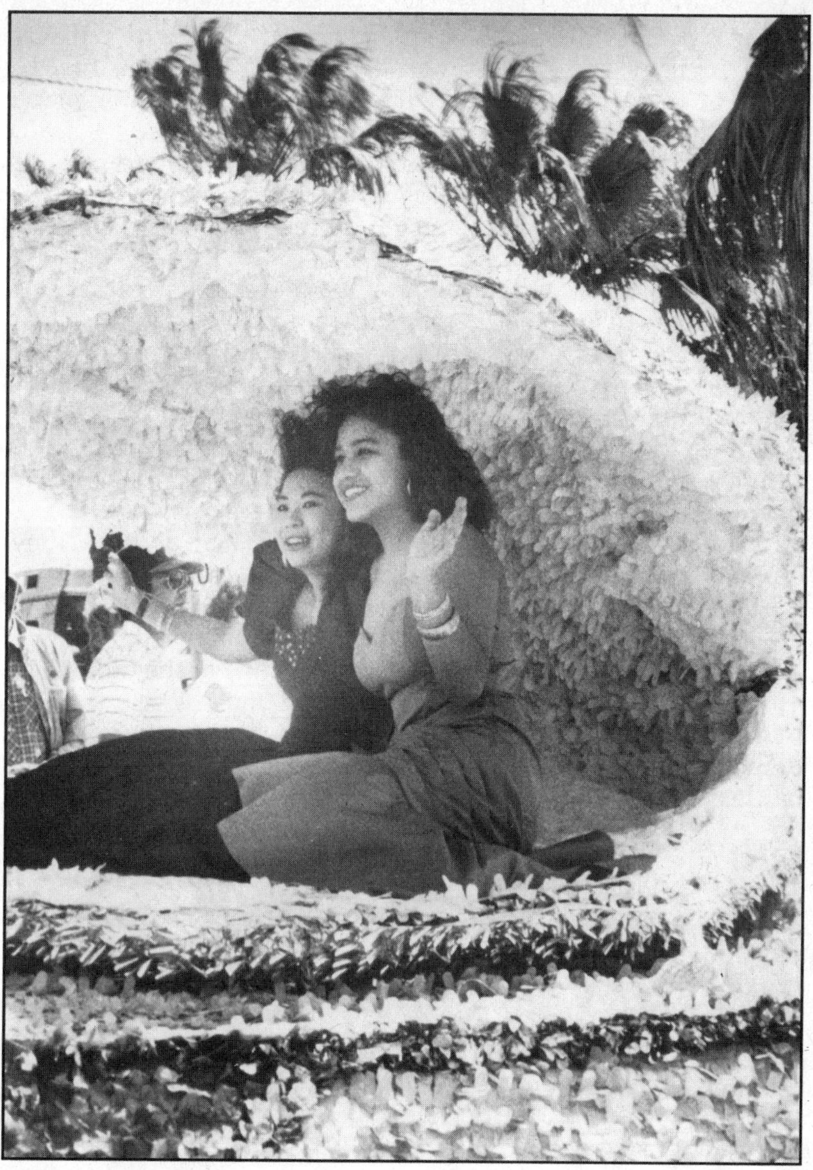

Young women wave from an oyster shell in the Fulton Oyster Fest parade. Photo by Dawn Albright.

squares next to the courthouse. The town is best known for its place in history as the "Lexington of Texas," where the first battle in Texas' war for independence from Mexico took place.

A little bitty old cannon is the focus of this spirited festival. When American settlers came to Gonzales, then a part of Mexico, in the 1820s and 1830s, they needed a weapon against Indian attacks. So the Mexican government gave them a small cannon.

When the Texas settlers began talking of revolt against Mexico, the government decided it wanted the cannon back and sent troops to Gonzales to reclaim it. The Texans weren't about to give up their gun, so they buried it in a peach orchard and sent for Texan reinforcements.

When they were ready to fight, the Texans unearthed the cannon, mounted it on a small wagon and hoisted a flag made from a wedding dress, with a picture of the cannòn and the taunting inscription, "Come And Take It." Then, at night, they crossed the Guadalupe River to the Mexican camp, fired the cannon and chased the soldiers away.

Activities include a parade, dance, arts and crafts fair, food booths, canoe races and a 10K run. You can visit the pioneer village living history center, a compound of eight historic buildings moved to the site for preservation. You can watch demonstrations of heritage arts and a reenactment of the battle.

Lufkin
Texas Forest Festival
Fourth weekend in September
Angelina County Chamber of Commerce, P.O. Box 1606, Lufkin 75902, 409/634-6644
Admission: $2

In the forest of East Texas, you'll find an old-fashioned celebration of food, music and fun. A main event of this festival is a cook-off, the Southern Hushpuppy Olympics. Any of you who've never tasted a hushpuppy should visit Lufkin in September, because it's a great southern tradition.

It's basically deep fried corn meal, which can be seasoned many ways. They're usually served up with fried catfish, cole slaw and beans.

Activities include a street dance, arts and crafts fair, fun run, old time fiddler's competition, food booths, carnival, a quilting and canning show, and lumberjack competition. Live entertainment incudes clogging, bands, singers and gymnasts.

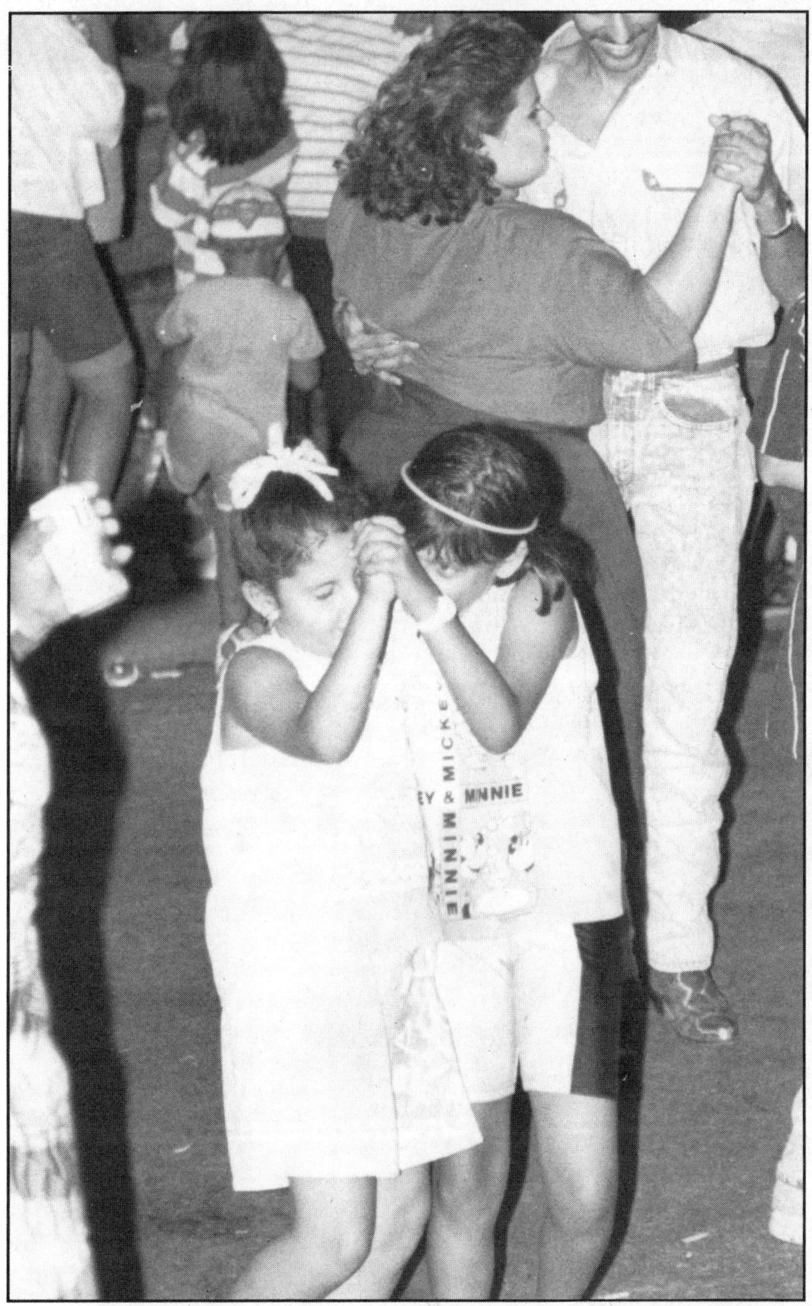

Kids and grown-ups enjoy the El Campo Grande Day street dance. *El Campo Leader-News* photo by Mark Thompson.

Devine
Devine Fall Festival
Last weekend in September
Greater Devine Chamber of Commerce, 200 E. Hondo Ave., Devine 78016, 512/663-2739

People in Devine take time in the fall to visit and mark the harvest with this event. The festival features a parade, a dance, arts and crafts by local artisans, a youth rodeo, music by local bands, a chili cook-off, and games.

El Campo
Grande Day
Last Saturday in September
El Campo Chamber of Commerce, P.O. Box 446, El Campo 77437, 409/543-2713
Admission: free

Just about everyone in this coastal prairie town comes out to Alamo Park for Grande Day. Festivities include an arts and crafts fair, egg toss tournament, beer garden, carnival, food booths featuring everything from tacos to brownies, and live entertainment on an outdoor stage. Contests include jalapeño eating, frozen yogurt eating and banana eating. A street dance at night tops it all off.

★

OCTOBER

Jasper
Jasper Fall Fest and Indian Summer Arts and Crafts Festival
First weekend in October
Jasper Chamber of Commerce, 246 E. Milam, Jasper 75951
409/384-2762
Admission: free

The Fall Fest combines an arts and crafts fair with the Deep East Texas State Fair for a busy weekend in Jasper. The three-day fair includes a quilt show, cooking and canning contests, a carnival and a rodeo playday featuring kid performers. These events take place at the rodeo grounds.

At the courthouse square on Saturday the arts and crafts fair offers visitors 100 booths with everything from wooden toys to handmade clothes. You can enjoy live music all day and a variety of food for sale. Shuttles usually run between the fairgrounds and the courthouse, stopping on the way for looks at historic buildings.

Livingston
Pine Cone Festival
First weekend in October
Polk County Chamber of Commerce, 516 W. Church, Livingston 77351, 409/327-4929
Admission: free

In the heart of the Piney Woods, Polk Countians pay tribute to the tree that grows tall and dense all around them. This event began as a folklife festival recalling the county's history, and now it's a full-blown annual bash that brings everyone out of the woods for food, fun and games.

They have a parade, a trail ride, an arts and crafts fair, a quilt show, food booths, an historical cabin, square dancing, and games.

Luckenbach
Ladies State Championship Chili Cook-off
First Saturday in October
Luckenbach General Store, 512/997-3224
Admission: free; fee for dance

Luckenbach hosts the women's championship cook-off for the state of Texas. About 140 cooking teams simmer their concoctions for several hours Saturday before the judging

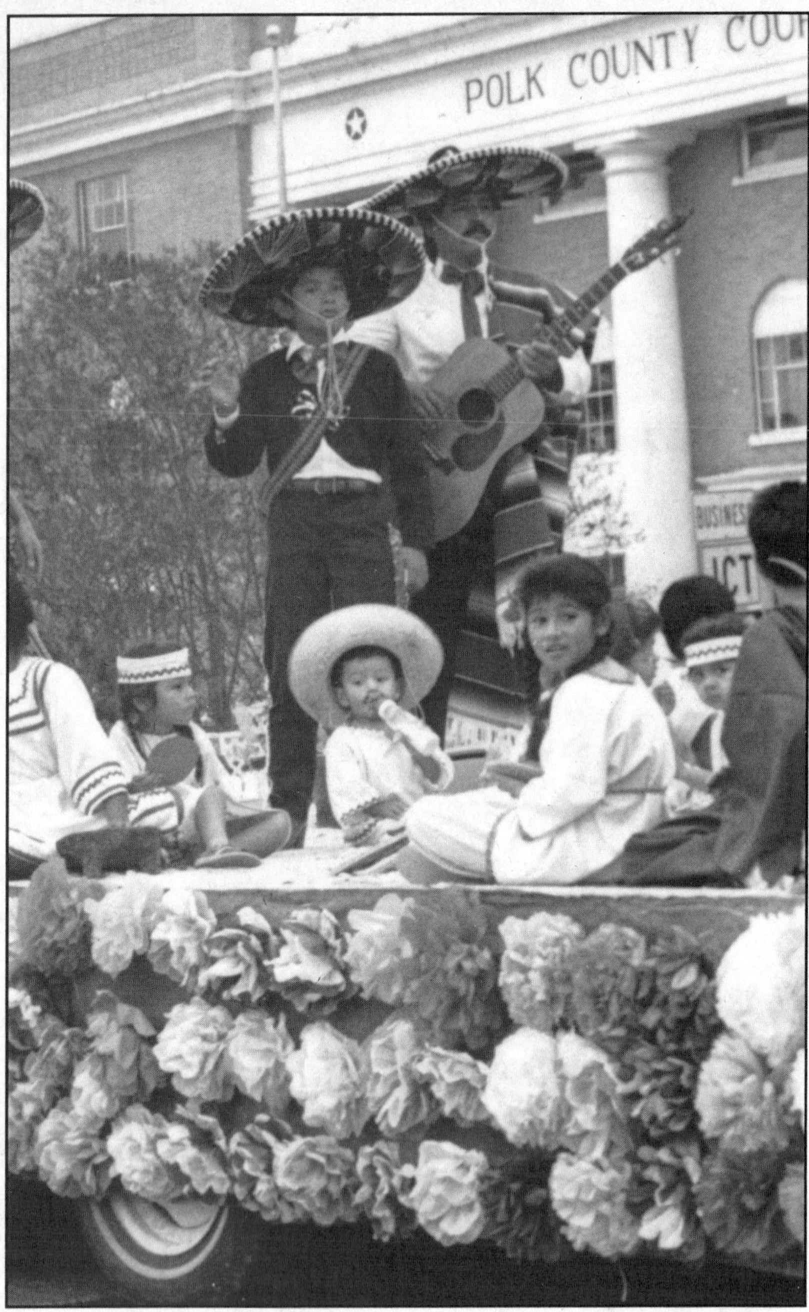

A parade float carries a Mexican theme during Livingston's Pine Cone Festival. Photo courtesy *Polk County Enterprise.*

takes place. Meanwhile, visitors enjoy games for kids and adults, including egg toss, facemaking and moseying contests. Folk musician Gary P. Nunn usually plays in the dance hall Saturday night.

The men's state championship chili cook-off is held in San Marcos the third weekend in September. Why separate cook-offs for women and men? Because the Chilympiad in San Marcos was founded by a group of men, and they decided not to allow women contestants.

The women's cook-off is decidedly less commercial, partly because of its location. Only a few people live in Luckenbach, a picturesque, laid-back place with a store, dance hall and blacksmith shop. The old general store, surrounded by ancient live oak trees, serves as the main attraction, where people gather for dominoes, music and beer.

Rockport
Rockport Seafair
Columbus Day weekend
Rockport-Fulton Chamber of Commerce, P.O. Box 1055, Rockport 78382, 512/729-6445; Toll free in Texas: 1-800-242-0071; outside Texas: 1-800-826-6441; or Rockport Seafair, Inc. 512/729-3312
Admission: free

October is a great month to visit the sea in Texas, when the water is still warm, but the air has cooled since summer. About 25,000 people swarm to Rockport for Seafair, a celebration of the ocean and the food it provides.

The fun includes plenty of water sports, as well as crab races and a crab beauty contest. Other activities include a parade, live bands, Miss Seafair pageant, a kiddie carnival, arts and crafts and food booths.

Palacios
Palacios Bayfest
First weekend in October
Palacios Chamber of Commerce, P.O. Box 774, Palacios 77465, 512/972-2615
Admission: free

This starts with a Friday night dance and continues Saturday with an all day celebration on the bay. There's a fiddler's contest, a barbecue cook-off, a 3-mile run, food, entertainment, and arts and crafts. A nighttime dance in the pavilion over the water concludes the festivities.

Wharton
Wharton Fest on the Colorado
First weekend in October
Wharton Chamber of Commerce, P.O. Box 868, Wharton 77488, 409/532-1862
Admission: free

Wharton's courthouse square comes alive for two days of food, fun and entertainment during Wharton Fest. A craft show, antique show, food booths, carnival, live entertainment and a dance attract fun-seekers. The Wharton County Historical Museum is open both days. This facility features exhibits on ranching, cotton and rice farming, historical figures and the settlement and growth of the area.

Winedale
Winedale Oktoberfest
First weekend in October
Winedale Historical Center, P.O. Box 11, Round Top 78954, 409/278-3530
Admission: $2 adult, 50 cents students

The Winedale and Round Top area was settled by German immigrants to Texas, so this traditional German holiday is important there. This festival includes plenty of German food, live music, dancers, and pioneer craft demonstrations. You can tour the historic houses and barns of Winedale and visit the Round Top Antique Show and Square Fair while you're there.

Winnie
Texas Rice Festival
First weekend in October
Winnie Area Chamber of Commerce, P.O. Box 147, Winnie 77665, 409/296-2231
Admission: $1

This giant party pays tribute to one of Southeast Texas' major crops — rice. Most people don't think of rice when they think of Texas, but we produce more rice than any other state, including California. With plenty of rain and a warm climate, the coastal plain is ideal for growing rice.

Activities include rice judging, rice milling, and rice eating and cooking contests. There are also two parades, five dances, an arts and crafts fair, a carnival, live entertainment, food booths, an old time fiddling contest, a goose calling contest, and a king and queen contest.

Floresville
Peanut Festival
Second weekend in October
Floresville Chamber of Commerce, P.O. Box 220, Floresville 78114, 512/393-3105, ask for chamber of commerce
Admission: free

In appreciation of Wilson County farmers, the citizens put on a big jubilee revolving around the peanut crop. You can see a peanut thrashing and taste homemade peanut butter and candy.

There's a parade, two street dances, contests, an arts and crafts fair, entertainment, food booths, queen coronation, carnival, and auction.

Fredericksburg
Oktoberfest
First weekend in October
Fredericksburg Chamber of Commerce, P.O. Box 506, Fredericksburg 78624, 512/997-6523 or Oktoberfest office, 512/997-4810
Admission: $4 to $5

Oktoberfest started in Munich, Germany in 1810 to celebrate the engagement of Crown Prince Ludwig to Baroness Theresa. This became an annual celebration, and when German immigrants came to America, they brought the tradition with them. Fredericksburg's Oktoberfest features arts, crafts, food, music, dancing, beer, children's entertainment and contests.

Bay City
Lion's Club Rice Festival
Second week in October
Bay City Chamber of Commerce, P.O. Box 768, Bay City 77404, 409/245-8333
Admission: free

Bay City's rice festival features a Saturday morning downtown parade, an arts and crafts fair, a carnival and food booths. Rice cook-off judging takes place Wednesday before the festival, and recipes are available after the winners are announced on Friday. Most of Saturday's activities take place at the fairgrounds.

Cuero
Turkeyfest
Second weekend in October

Cuero Chamber of Commerce, 103 N. Esplanade, Cuero 77954, 512/275-6351, 275-2112
Admission: free

The festivities begin Saturday with the Great Gobbler Gallop, a turkey race between Cuero's Ruby Begonia and Paycheck from Worthington, Minnesota. Thousands of spectators line the street to cheer Cuero's turkey in the race. The birds also compete in an annual race in Minnesota.

The rest of the fun includes a parade, 5K run, chili cook-off, barbecue cook-off, a dance, a carnival, and horseshoe and washer tournaments. You can peruse the arts and crafts area and sample goodies from the food booths while enjoying live entertainment.

Falfurrias
Fiesta del Campo
Columbus Day weekend
Falfurrias Chamber of Commerce, P.O. Box 476, Falfurrias 78355, 512/325-3333
Admission: free

About 10,000 people get together in Falfurrias to celebrate the countryside with games, a dance, trail ride, arts and crafts fair, music and food booths. There's also a chili cook-off, horseshoe tournament and carnival rides.

Uvalde
Cactus Jack Festival
Second weekend in October
Uvalde Chamber of Commerce, P.O. Box 706, Uvalde 78802, 512/278-3361
Admission: fee for some events

Since 1975, Uvalde has remembered former vice president John Nance "Cactus Jack" Garner with this festival. Garner, a native of Uvalde, was vice president of the United States under Franklin D. Roosevelt from 1933 to 1941.

The event includes a parade, dance, contests, arts and crafts, stage show and food booths.

Beeville
Western Week
Third week in October
Bee County Chamber of Commerce, P.O. Box 4099, Beeville 78104, 512/358-3267; Western Week Inc., 512/358-0502 or 358-8080

Admission: $2 adult

Beeville goes West for four days with a parade, dance and rodeo. You'll also find an arts and crafts fair, contests, live entertainment and food booths.

Buchanan Dam
Dam Birthday Party
Mid-October
Lake Buchanan Chamber of Commerce, P.O. Box 282, Buchanan Dam 78609, 512/793-2803
Admission: free except for boat cruises

The community of Buchanan Dam developed in the 1930s as the dam was built to create Lake Buchanan. Held in a park next to the dam, festivities usually include plenty of music, arts and crafts, food booths, dancing, concerts, light shows or fireworks, tours of the generating plant, boat cruises along the dam, and games.

Yorktown
Yorktown Annual Western Days Celebration
Third full weekend in October
Yorktown Chamber of Commerce, P.O. Box 488, Yorktown 78164, 512/564-2661
Admission: free

Yorktown's Western Days has a children's parade and a grand parade. They also have dances, a Little Mr. and Miss pageant, a fiddler's contest, trail ride, arts and crafts, food booths, and a carnival. Chili, bean and barbecue cook-offs also take place during the weekend.

Boerne
Oktoberfest
Third Saturday of October
Boerne Area Chamber of Commerce, 1 Main Plaza, Boerne 78006, 512/249-8000
Admission: free

Boerne's Oktoberfest combines food and physical activity. Besides all the great vittles, they have 21-, 45-, 60-, and 100-mile bike races. You can dance all day to the German bands. There's also storytelling, a dance, contests, arts and crafts, food booths, and a starving artist show.

Flatonia
Czhilispiel

An exhibitor demonstrates chair caning at the General Sam Houston Folklife Festival in Huntsville. Photo courtesy General Sam Houston Folklife Festival.

Fourth weekend in October
Flatonia Chamber of Commerce, P.O. Box 651, Flatonia 78941, 512/865-3920
Admission: free

Flatonia, in the heart of German/Czech country, boasts the world's largest tented beer garden at Czhilispiel. And under this tent, you can listen to well-known Texas country and polka bands. Of course, there's a chili cook-off, as well as barbecue beef and pork cook-offs. Other diversions include a parade, street dances, contests, arts and crafts, and a carnival.

Sinton
Old Fiddler's Festival
Last weekend in October
Sinton Chamber of Commerce, P.O. Box 217, Sinton 78387, 512/364-2307
Admission: free

Sinton started the fiddler's contest before 1950, adding the other activities in 1976. Now they have a parade, cabrito and chili cook-offs, a dance, arts and crafts fair, 5K and 10K runs, team roping, music, and games.

New Braunfels
Wurstfest
Begins the first Friday after the last Wednesday in October, and lasts 10 days
Wurstfest Association, P.O. Box 310309, New Braunfels 78131, 1-800-221-4369 or 512/625-9167
Admission: $4 to grounds, including two entertainment tents; $2 to enter Wursthall

Wurstfest, which celebrates sausage making and German heritage, attracts about 130,000 visitors each year. The Wurstfest grounds include a large building, tents and a park area.

It started in 1961 as a local sausage promotion for the townspeople, and has grown to become one of the biggest sausage festivals in the world.

There's sausage galore, other food, beer, music, and dances each night. Festivities begin with the Wurst Navy floating parade on the clear blue Comal River. The Comal, by the way, is the world's shortest river, only about three miles long from its source to where it joins the Guadalupe. But it's not a mere stream — the spring-fed waterway has an average flow of 200- to 300-cubic feet per second. And the water from Comal Spring stays about 70 degrees all year.

Activities include a major horseshoe tournament, German bands, a heritage exhibit, and an old-time melodrama.

NOVEMBER

Carrizo Springs
Brush Country Days
First or second weekend in November
Dimmit County Chamber of Commerce, 107 West Nopal, Carrizo Springs 78834, 512/876-5205
Admission: $1 adult; kids under 12 free

People from all over Dimmit County come to this festival, which features a parade, a dance, an arts and crafts fair, and 5K and 10K runs. You can also see a ranch rodeo, mock gunfighters and dance groups. Local bands play in the pavilion throughout the afternoon.

George West
Storyfest
First Saturday in November
George West Chamber of Commerce, P.O. Box 359, George West 78022, 512/449-2915
Admission: free

This festival features two stages where amateur and professional storytellers spin their yarns. Live music, primarily Texas folk music, entertains visitors throughout the day. In 1989 the featured musician was Robert Earl Keen Jr. There's an arts and crafts fair, food booths and a street dance.

Rob Schneider, a George West lawyer, believed a celebration such as Storyfest would help preserve the art of storytelling. His great-great uncle, Rocky Reagan, was a renowned storyteller in town. Even J. Frank Dobie, the great Texas storyteller, used to come to Reagan for stories, Schneider said.

Storytelling seems to pervade the George West community. "Just about anybody around here will tell a story," Schneider said. "You can't go down to the coffee shop without hearing some kind of story."

Bridge City
Bridge City Days
First weekend in November
Bridge City Chamber of Commerce, 150 W. Roundbunch, Bridge City 77611, 409/735-5671
Admission: free

Bridge City Days, celebrated since 1969, includes a parade, bike race, live music, tiny tot pageant, contests, arts and crafts, country music talent show and food booths. Most events are held outdoors at the Bridge City Community Center.

★

DECEMBER

Raymondville
Fun Fiesta
First weekend in December
Raymondville Chamber of Commerce, P.O. Box 746, Raymondville 78580, 512/689-3171
Admission: free

In South Texas, the weather's still balmy in December, so the folks in Raymondville welcome the season with a parade, bean cook-off, fajita cook-off, arts and crafts, food booths and a 5K run. For music, they usually round up a mariachi band and some old time fiddlers.

Mission
Tourist Fest
Second weekend of December
Mission Chamber of Commerce, P.O. Box 431, Mission 78572, 512/585-2727
Admission: free

Designed especially for Winter Texans, those folks who spend the winter months in South Texas instead of in the chilly north, this festival presents a panorama of South Texas culture with music, dancing, food, and an arts and crafts fair.

The three-day event takes place downtown in Lomita Plaza. You'll see square and round dance exhibitions, clogging, ballet folklorico and mariachi bands. Music includes bluegrass, country and western, jazz and choral. Other events include a 5K walk, a health fair, and poinsettia show.

★

West Texas and Panhandle

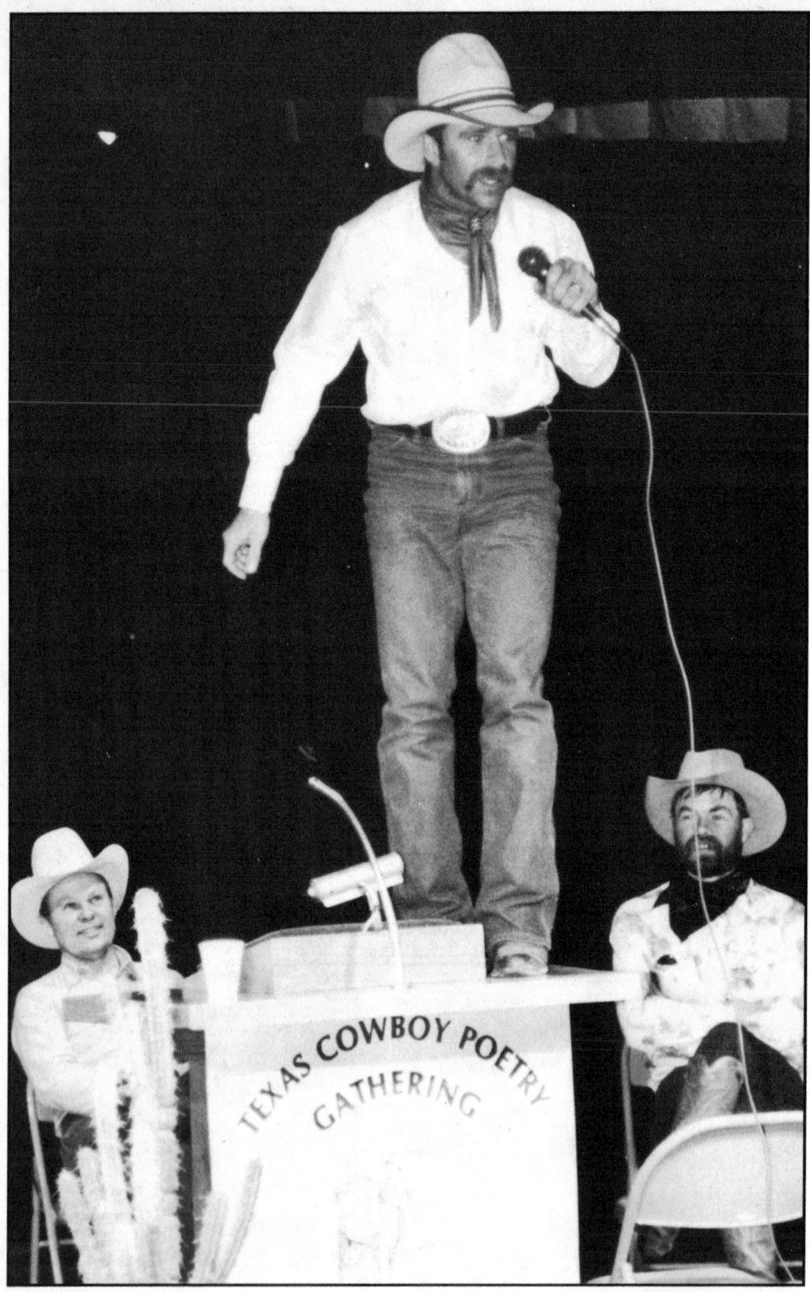

Nyle Henderson recites a poem during the Texas Cowboy Poetry Gathering in Alpine. Photo by Barbara Richerson, Sul Ross University News and Information.

MARCH

Alpine
Texas Cowboy Poetry Gathering
First weekend in March
Alpine Chamber of Commerce, P.O. Box 209, Alpine 79831, 915/837-2326
Admission: free

Real cowboys, young and old, who work on ranches and write poetry, attend this festival and share their work with other cowboy poets and the public. This event at Sul Ross State University, begun in 1986, starts Thursday night with an open poetry reading. Friday and Saturday feature poetry readings all day, music in the late afternoon, chuckwagon suppers and campfire sessions. The daytime readings are scheduled according to theme or subject matter, such as humor, ranch life or storytelling.

You can also see demonstrations by cowboy craftsmen of saddlemaking, bootmaking, and other skills used in ranching. You also may hear recitations of poetry written by cowboys long dead.

Sweetwater
World's Largest Rattlesnake Round-up
Second weekend in March
Sweetwater Chamber of Commerce, P.O. Box 1148, Sweetwater 79556, 915/235-5488
Admission to coliseum: $5

The Sweetwater Rattlesnake Round-up began 31 years ago to decrease the rattlesnake population that threatened livestock on area ranches. Now, the annual event is famous worldwide and attracts about 35,000 visitors each year. Sponsored by the Sweetwater Jaycees, most activities take place in the Nolan County Coliseum.

Rattlesnake handlers demonstrate snake milking techniques for visitors. Yes, they actually "milk" the venom from the rattlesnakes, which is used in cancer research and as an antidote for snakebite victims.

The three-day event includes a paradeThursday afternoon, a dance, contests, rattlesnake hunts, arts and crafts, food booths (including cooked rattlesnake), and a 10K run the rest of the weekend.

Shamrock
St. Patrick's Day
Weekend nearest March 17
St. Patrick's Association, P.O. Box 588, Shamrock 79079, 806/256-2501
Admission: free except for banquet and dance

This town hosts a parade with 100 entries and 15,000 people. The one-day festival in honor of Ireland's patron saint began in 1938 and now attracts 10,000 people to the Panhandle each year. A band director started the festival, so activities still include a band performance after the parade.

In addition to the parade, the people of Shamrock organize a beard growing contest, sheepdog trials, barrel racing, team roping, 5K run, one-mile fun run, Miss Irish Rose contest and Miss Shamrock contest. You'll find a banquet that starts off the festivities, a chili cook-off, water polo, teen and adult dances, and a carnival.

The town boasts a piece of the Blarney Stone in Elmore Park, which the chamber of commerce imported from Ireland in 1948. If you kiss the Blarney Stone, you'll receive the gift of gab.

★

APRIL

Ballinger
Texas State Festival of Ethnic Cultures and Arts and Crafts Show
Last weekend in April
Ballinger Chamber of Commerce, P.O. Box 577, Ballinger 76821, 915/365-2333
Admission: free

Begun as a bicentennial project, this event now draws about 8,000 visitors. They have a parade, dance, contests, arts and crafts fair, live entertainment, and food booths.

Cisco
Folklife Festival
Last weekend in April
Cisco Chamber of Commerce, 309 Conrad Hilton Ave., Cisco 76437, 817/442-2537
Admission: $1.50

This event, dedicated to preserving pioneer skills, takes place next to the first hotel ever built by Conrad Hilton. Now restored, the building usually hosts a quilt or crafts show during the festival.

Activities include a Saturday morning parade, trail ride with breakfast at the end, children's games, music, food booths, arts and crafts and a Saturday night dance.

You can see continuous demonstrations of pioneer skills such as corn grinding, basket weaving and tatting. Entertainment includes an antique clothing style show, local choirs, gymnasts and dance groups.

Turkey
Bob Wills Day
Last weekend in April
Bob Wills Foundation, P.O. Box 67, Turkey 79261, call city hall at 806/423-1033
Admission to some events

This hometown tribute to the King of Western Swing, the late Bob Wills, features plenty of live music. There's a fiddler's contest, free outdoor concert Saturday afternoon, dances, downtown parade, and a barbecue lunch at the Bob Wills Center. Some of the former Texas Playboys, Bob Wills' band, often attend the event.

You can see the Bob Wills monument, visit the Bob Wills Museum, see arts and crafts at the Bob Wills Center, and hear music and eat in the Bob Wills Cafeteria. You can watch movies and television shows in which Bob Wills appeared.

MAY

Iraan
Alley Oop Day
May or June of odd-numbered years
Iraan Chamber of Commerce, P.O. Box 153, Iraan 79744, 915/639-2628
Admission: free

The creator of the Alley Oop cartoon strip, V.T. Hamlin, lived in little old Iraan, Texas, where he worked as a geologist for an oil company. Folks say the prehistoric nature of the terrain in Pecos County inspired the creation of Alley Oop. So now they hold a festival to honor Hamlin every other year.

Activities include a parade, a dance, golf cart races, pet shows, and a chili cook-off. There's also an arts and crafts fair and a variety of live entertainment provided by local musicians and dancers.

Lamesa
May Fun-Fest
First weekend in May
Lamesa Area Chamber of Commerce, P.O. Drawer J, Lamesa 79331, 806/872-2181
Admission: free

Visitors to Lamesa will find a bicycle parade, food booths, arts and crafts, cake walks, pie and watermelon eating contests, dog shows and baby contests.

Vernon
Doan's May Picnic
First Saturday in May

Vernon Chamber of Commerce, P.O. Box 1538, Vernon, 76384, 817/552-2564.
Admission: free

This community picnic has been held every May Day since 1884 in Watt's Grove on the Red River. A local school sells barbecue, but most people bring a picnic lunch, spread a blanket on the ground and relax for the day. The main event is the crowning of the king and queen. Tip Igou, president of the Doan's May Picnic Association, explained the royalty must be descendants of original settlers of Wilbarger County.

Although most picnickers are locals, travelers are welcome. One year, a group of Italians touring the United States on motorcycles stopped by, Igou said.

Seymour
Fish Day
First Monday in May (part of weekend festivities)
Seymour Chamber of Commerce, P.O. Box 1379, Seymour 76380, 817/888-2921
Admission to some events

This annual three-day event culminates on Monday when everyone closes up shop and heads out to Lake Kemp for games and food. They have a dance, a fish fry contest, fishing, boating, volleyball, a log roll, a tug of war, a queen contest, arts and crafts, and food booths. They've been holding this event for more than 60 years.

It's true, all the businesses in Seymour close that Monday. Of course, the U.S. Post Office stays open, as well as gas stations and food stores.

Fort Stockton
Cinco de Mayo Celebration
May 5
Fort Stockton Chamber of Commerce, P.O. Box C, Fort Stockton 79735, 915/336-2264
Admission: $2

May 5 marks the day in 1865 when the Mexican army repelled a French invasion at the city of Puebla.

Fort Stockton's festival celebrates Hispanic culture with conjunto and Tejano music, ballet folklorico performed by children, and a street dance. It usually starts in the late afternoon and goes until after midnight. Other attractions include a talent stage, arts and crafts, and food booths.

Abilene
Western Heritage Classic
Second Friday and Saturday in May
Abilene Convention and Visitors Council, P.O. Box 2281, Abilene 79604, 1-800-727-7704
Admission: $6 to grounds and rodeo

This Western weekend festures ranch rodeo with real cowboys competing in real ranching events. Each night after the rodeo, there's a dance and a cowboy breakfast. Other activities include matched cowboy horse races, harness driving competition, cowboy poetry and music performances, a chuckwagon cook-off, and a western art show.

Santa Anna
Fun-tier Days
Second weekend in May
Santa Anna Chamber of Commerce, P.O. Box 275, Santa Anna, 76878, 915/348-3535.
Admission: free

The folks in Santa Anna organize a wool demonstration in which sheep shearers, spinners and weavers team up to show you how wool is processed from start to finish.

Other activities include an antique tractor show, a Maypole dance, a parade, a dance, an arts and crafts fair, a stage show, food booths, and a fun run.

Vernon
Santa Rosa Round-up
Third weekend in May
Vernon Chamber of Commerce, P.O. Box 1538, Vernon 76384, 817/552-2564
Admission to rodeo

This is mostly a rodeo with arts and crafts, food booths and a barbecue cook-off. The rodeo runs Wednesday through Saturday.

Eldorado
World Championship Cowboy Campfire Cooking and Pasture Roping
Memorial Day Weekend
Schleicher County Chamber of Commerce, P.O. Box 1155, Eldorado, 76936, 915/853-3109.

This festival celebrating the origin of the cowboy features a unique dog barking contest. Main attractions include the campfire cook-off, pasture and other roping competition, a fiddler's contest, an art show, and a cocktail party.

JUNE

Big Spring
Heart of the City Festival
First weekend in June
Big Spring Chamber of Commerce, P.O. Box 1391, Big Spring 79720, 915/263-7641
Admission: free

If you're near Big Spring in June, make a visit to this festival held downtown by the courthouse square. The event offers arts and crafts booths, live music all day, a chili cook-off, food booths, children's games, and a street dance. Other entertainment includes face painting, belly dancers, and mock gunfights.

Throckmorton
Pioneer Day
First or second weekend in June
Throckmorton Chamber of Commerce, P.O. Box 711, Throckmorton 76083, 817/849-2661

This festival grew out of Throckmorton's celebration of its 100th birthday in 1958. It features a barbecue lunch on the courthouse square, buggy rides, tours of the museum and water plant, a parade, dance, contests, arts and crafts, a stage show, and food booths.

Baird
Baird Trades Day
First Saturday in June
Baird Chamber of Commerce, P.O. Box 846, Baird 79504, 915/854-2003
Admission: free except for dance and barbecue

Most activities take place on the sidewalks of downtown Baird, although there's a fiddler's contest in the Opry Theater. This classic example of a small town festival includes a street dance, food booths, arts and crafts, 5K run, bubble gum blowing contest, pie baking contest and tricycle races.

There's also a flea market, quilt display, antique tractor and car show, square dancing, gymnastics, a barbecue lunch and a rodeo. The folks in Baird have been putting this on since 1973.

Brackettville
Frontier Fair
First weekend in June
Kinney County Chamber of Commerce, P.O. Box 386, Brackettville 78832, 512/563-2466
Admission: free

This old-time county fair brings together all the folks in this sparsely populated area for a weekend of fun. They put on a parade, a dance, an arts and crafts fair, and a variety of games. Sometimes there's a tortilla tossing contest, and always plenty to choose from among the food booths. The volunteer fire department hosts pumper races, which involves a team hooking up a hose to a tank truck and making the water flow as quickly as they can.

While you're in Brackettville, you might drive out to see Alamo Village, the Western movie set built for The Alamo, starring John Wayne. The set, six miles north of town, looks just like what you'd see in a movie, complete with church, saloon and hotel. They still use the place to make movies. During summer months, there's entertainment, but otherwise, you can check out the shops.

Miami
National Cow Calling Contest
First Saturday in June
Miami Chamber of Commerce, P.O. Box 456, Miami 79059, 806/868-3191
Admission: free

If you're in the neighborhood, drive on over to Miami for an afternoon of listening to people holler from an outdoor stage. These folks moo, low and yell until the judges, standing some distance away, decide whose voice would best bring the cows home.

The three contestant categories in cow calling are men, women and grandmothers. The older women said it wouldn't

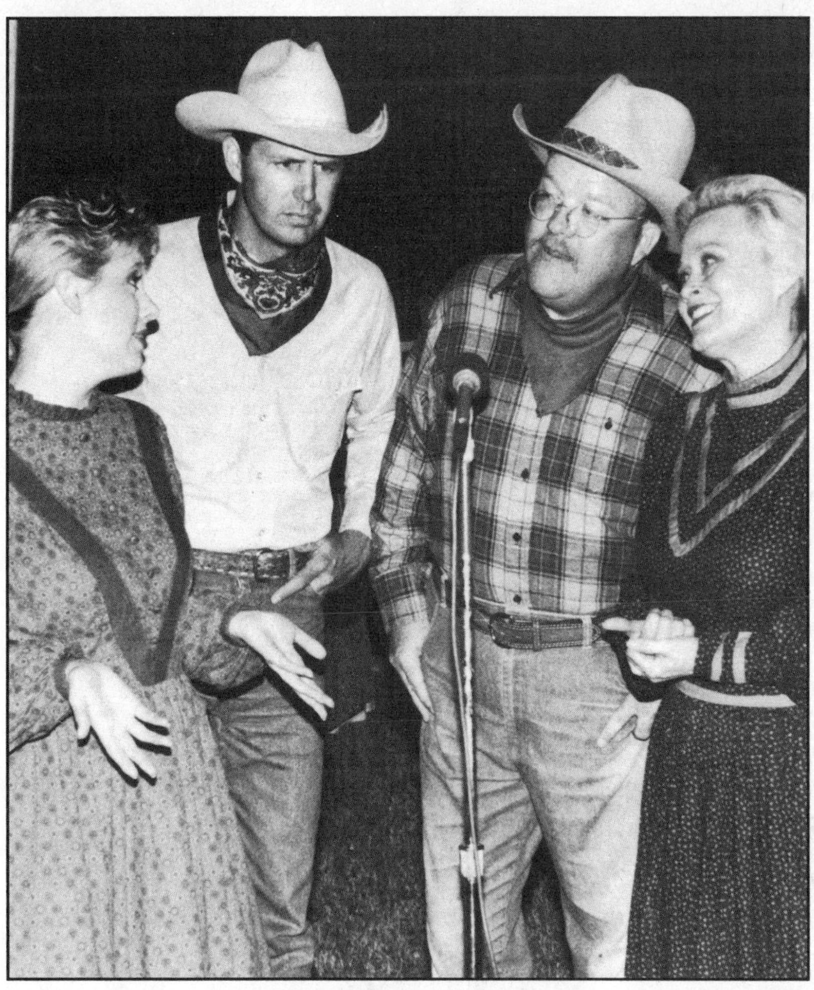

Singers Sara Maxey, Randall Palmore, James Carroll and Sandra Fox perform in the Fort Griffin Fandangle in Albany. Photo courtesy *Albany News*.

be fair to the younger ones to compete in the same class, explained Judy Cook, of the Miami Chamber of Commerce. This Panhandle town has been holding the Cow Calling Contest since around 1950.

Besides the Cow Calling, the town puts on the Frontier Follies, a local talent show, Friday night. On Saturday, there's a barbecue lunch before the Calling gets underway. You can check out the arts and crafts booths Saturday afternoon, and go to the dance Saturday night.

While Miami has no motels, there is an RV park. The nearest motel is in Canadian, 23 miles away.

Spearman
Hansford Round-up Celebration
First weekend in June
Spearman Chamber of Commerce, P.O. Box 161, Spearman 79081, 806/659-5555
Admission: free except for rodeo

This has a parade, street dance, stage show, food booths, rodeo, a gunfight and dancers on Main Street, a barbecue, biathlon, and a carnival.

Albany
Fort Griffin Fandangle
Last two weekends in June — Thursday through Saturday evenings
Albany Chamber of Commerce, P.O. Box 185, Albany 76430, 915/762-2525
Admission: $3 to $10 for performance tickets

A historical drama about the Albany area, the Fort Griffin Fandangle is performed outdoors in a natural amphitheatre by a cast of 300 local people. Robert Nail, a teacher, wrote it in 1938 for the town's high school seniors to perform. The town liked it, and has put on the show every year since then. Each night (six performances total) the audience fills all 1,500 seats.

Besides the evening entertainment, other events include a parade, a nightly barbecue dinner on the courthouse square, tours, an arts and crafts fair, and food booths. The Old Jail Museum in Albany houses works by famous artists, including Picasso, Modigliani, Henry Moore and Paul Klee.

Canyon
TEXAS Musical Drama
Mid-June through late August

TEXAS, Box 268, Canyon 79015, 806/655-2181
Admission: ticket prices range from $6 to $12; lower prices for kids

Just outside Canyon, in Palo Duro Canyon State Park, this nightly (except Sunday) performance attracts thousands of people each year. A professional cast of 80 entertains the audience in an outdoor theatre with song and dance telling the story of the settlement of the Panhandle. Shows often sell out ahead of time, so it's a good idea to buy advance tickets. A barbecue dinner is served each night before the performance from 6:30 to 8 p.m.

Dumas
Dogie Days Celebration
Second or third weekend in June
Dumas Chamber of Commerce, P.O. Box 735, Dumas 79029, 806/935-2123
Admission: free except for barbecue

Hosted by the Dumas Noon Lions Club, this festival includes a parade, carnival, western and teen dances, barbecue and food booths. Your barbecue ticket buys a chance to win a pickup truck, in a drawing held the last day of the festival.

Perryton
Springfest
First weekend in June
Perryton-Ochiltree Chamber of Commerce, P.O. Drawer 789, Perryton 79070, 806/435-6575
Admission: $2 adult, $1 for kids

Springfest takes place at Wolf Creek Park and features an evening concert followed by a dance. Other activities include bicycle races, sports contests, game and food booths, a horseshoe tournament, tug of war, and a carnival. There's a chicken, brisket and rib cook-off, as well as a Texas pinto bean cook-off.

Van Horn
Frontier Days and Big Country Celebration
Third weekend in June
Van Horn Chamber of Commerce, P.O. Box 721, Van Horn 79855, 915/283-2043
Admission to some activities

This festival, in existence since 1957, features a parade, a dance, contests, square dance performances, food booths, and an arts and crafts fair.

Pecos
Night in Old Pecos
Last Tuesday in June
Pecos Chamber of Commerce, P.O. Box 27, Pecos, 79772, 915/445-2406
Admission: free

Night in Old Pecos starts off Western Week, which all leads up to the West of the Pecos Rodeo, known as the world's first rodeo. (See July entry.) Night in Old Pecos features a dance, arts and crafts, contests, a stage show, and food booths.

Sudan
Pioneer Independence Day Celebration
Last Saturday in June
Sudan Chamber of Commerce, P.O. Box 224, Sudan 79371, 806/227-2564
Admission: free except for barbecue

This one-day festival has a parade, street dance, an arts and crafts fair, food booths, kids games and a barbecue meal.

★

JULY

Pecos
West of the Pecos Rodeo
First four days in July
Pecos Chamber of Commerce, P.O. Box 27, Pecos 79772, 915/445-2406
Admission: $4 to $6 for rodeo seats

Known as the world's first rodeo, this event was first held in 1883. Besides roping and riding, there's a parade, trail ride, dance every night after the rodeo, a pageant, Western art show and sale, arts and crafts and food booths.

It all starts a week earlier, on the last Tuesday in June, with Night in Old Pecos (see June entry), which kicks off Western Week.

Clarendon
Saint's Roost Celebration
July 4th weekend
Clarendon Chamber of Commerce, P.O. Box 730, Clarendon 79266, 806/874-2421
Admission to rodeo

Clarendon used to be known as Saint's Roost, a name sarcastically used by area cowboys. The town's founder, Methodist minister L.H. Carhart, forbade gambling and alcohol. So besides celebrating the Fourth of July, the citizens also recognize their history with this festival.

Rodeos all three nights of the celebration are each followed by a dance with old-time country music. On July 4, there's a parade, contests, arts and crafts, stage show, food booths, turtle race, old-timer's reunion, and a barbecue cookout. They've been celebrating Independence Day in this way since 1878.

Colorado City
July Fourthfest and Fly-in
July 4
Colorado City Chamber of Commerce, P.O. Box 242, Colorado City 79512, 915/728-3403
Admission: free

Colorado City holds its July 4 festival in Ruddick Park with an arts and crafts fair, games, food booths, a hamburger supper in the evening and a fireworks display after sundown.

Those who want a little exercise can enter the 5K run, 1-mile fun run or the 1-mile walk.

The Fly-in, which has been going on since 1962, features aerobatic stunts, a skydiving demonstration and airplane rides. Pilots who fly into the airport northwest of town in the morning receive a free breakfast. Other folks can eat for a fee, then have a look at the airplanes.

Fort Davis
Old Fashioned Fourth of July
July 4 and a weekend
Fort Davis Chamber of Commerce, P.O. Box 378, Fort Davis 79734, 915/426-3015
Admission: free

This festival features a parade, dance, tortilla toss, cantaloupe eating contest, live music all day, children's games, arts and crafts, food booths and roping.

Fort Stockton
Fourth of July Festival
July 4
Fort Stockton Chamber of Commerce, P.O. Box C, Fort Stockton 79735, 915/336-2264
Admission: free

They have a dance, live entertainment, contests, arts and crafts and food booths, all in James Ronney Park. At night, the local Jaycees put on a fireworks display.

The actual fort in Fort Stockton has been partially restored, so you can take either a self-guided or bus tour of the landmark.

Lamesa
July 4th Community Picnic
July 4
Lamesa Area Chamber of Commerce, P.O. Drawer J, Lamesa 79331, 806/872-2181
Admission: free

Activities include a dance, contests, arts and crafts, stage show, food booths and a volleyball tournament.

Merkel
Fun Day
July 4
Merkel Chamber of Commerce, P.O. Box 536, Merkel 79536,

915/928-5722
Admission: free
Fun Day, which takes place in Merkel's South Park, features live music by local bands, a variety of games, an arts and crafts fair, and food booths.

Monahans
July 4 Freedom Fair
July 4
Monahans Chamber of Commerce, P.O. Box 1040, Monahans 79756, 915/943-2187
Admission: free
Monahans celebrates Independence Day with a parade, arts and crafts contest, a fun run, games, music, and food.
Monahans Sandhills State Park features 3,800 acres of sand dunes, some of them 70 feet tall. The town's Million Barrel Museum features a large cement-lined hole in the ground built in 1928 to store a million barrels of oil. The plan didn't work, so now they use the tank for dances, barbecues and other large activities. The museum also has a collection of historic buildings and farm, ranch and railroad items.

Muleshoe
July 4 Celebration
July 4
Muleshoe Chamber of Commerce, 215 S. First, Muleshoe 79347, 806/272-4248
Admission: free
Muleshoe celebrates July 4 with a parade, street dance, cow patty bingo, games for kids and grown-ups, 10K and 2-mile runs, and arts and crafts. Of course, they have fireworks at night.

Ozona
Celebration on the Square
July 4
Ozona Chamber of Commerce, P.O. Box 1135, Ozona 76943, 915/392-3066
Admission: free
Ozona's July 4 celebration has a parade, arts and crafts, an apple pie bake-off, performances by the Sahawe Indian dancers at night, fireworks, food, games, entertainment and special displays in the historical museum.
The evening of July 3, everyone turns out for the Old Time

Beauty Pageant, the main event of which is men modeling old-fashioned swimsuits. The audience enjoys homemade ice cream and other entertainment.

Snyder
July 4th Celebration
July 4
Snyder Chamber of Commerce, P.O. Drawer CC, Snyder 79549, 915/573-3558
Admission: free

Snyder's salute to Independence Day features a fireworks display, parade, arts and crafts, stage show, carnival and food booths. Contests include washer pitching, hula hoop, and limbo.

Wheeler
July 4th Celebration
July 4
Wheeler Chamber of Commerce, P.O. Box 221, Wheeler 79096, 806/826-3408
Admission: free

Folks in Wheeler bring you such sights as skydivers, hot air balloons, a radio-controlled model plane airshow, and fireworks. Other activities include a fun run, street dance, turtle races, free swimming, volleyball, contests, stage show and food booths.

Seymour
Old Settlers Reunion and Rodeo
Second weekend in July
Seymour Chamber of Commerce, P.O. Box 1379, Seymour 76380, 817/888-2921
Admission to rodeo

This annual event began in 1896 after a retired cowboy named Jeff Scott came up with the idea of a cowboy's reunion. The first year, several thousand people showed up for the event, which included a free barbecue, a baseball game, a band concert, a grand ball, and a rodeo.

The second cowboy reunion, in 1897, featured Comanche Chief Quanah Parker and 500 Indians performing dances around a campfire for an audience of 10,000. The story goes that the Indians walked into Seymour on a Sunday morning while everyone was in church. When the worshipers saw the large crowd of Indians in the street, they poured out of the sanctuary doors, overwhelmed with curiosity.

Now known as the Old Settlers Reunion, the festival once again boasts Indian dancers. The major events take place on Thursday, starting with the Reunion. Then there's the election of the Old Settlers King and Queen, the parade, rodeo and dance. The arts and crafts show goes on during this time as well. The rodeo and dance also take place Friday and Saturday nights.

Levelland
Early Settlers Reunion
Second Saturday in July
Levelland Chamber of Commerce, 1101 Ave. H, Levèlland 79336, 806/894-3157
Admission: free

Folks in Levelland come out to see old friends and enjoy the parade, street dance, food booths and arts and crafts fair. There's also a dog show, horseshoe contest, stick horse race, washer pitching, all-day entertainment, and a quilt show. Most activities are held on the grounds of the Hockley County Courthouse.

Stanton
Martin County Old Settlers Reunion
Second Saturday in July
Martin County Chamber of Commerce, P.O. Box 614, Stanton 79782, 915/458-3350
Admission: free except for barbecue and homes tour

Started in 1930, this event has a parade, dance, barbecue at the city park, arts and crafts, food booths, contests, and open roping. Visitors can enjoy the Historical Museum, Old Jail, Old Convent, and the Old Texas Theatre.

Claude
Caprock Round-up
Third weekend in July
Claude Chamber of Commerce, P.O. Box 129, Claude 79019, 806/226-2221 (this is a drug store where the people can tell you about the festival)
Admission: free

Activities include a parade, dance, arts and crafts fair, live entertainment by dancers and musicians, and a free barbecue lunch. About 4,000 people attend the celebration.

Claude is just east of Amarillo and north of Palo Duro

Top photo: Christi Card performs in the air in a Salute to Esther Williams during the Fort Stockton Water Carnival. Photo by Phil Chamberlain/*Fort Stockton Pioneer.*

Bottom photo: Children create a sparkle of splashes in a performance during the Fort Stockton Water Carnival. Photo by Phil Chamberlain/*Fort Stockton Pioneer.*

Canyon, an essential stop for any traveler through the Panhandle.

Tulia, Kress and Happy
Swisher County Picnic
Weekend closest to July 17
Tulia Chamber of Commerce, P.O. Box 267, Tulia 79088, 806/995-4426
Admission: free except for barbecue meal

This countywide celebration, which began in 1900, includes a parade, dance, rodeo, barbecue meal, old-time fiddler's contest, antique car show, carnival, food booths, and live entertainment.

Fort Stockton
Water Carnival
Third weekend in July
Fort Stockton Chamber of Commerce, P.O. Box C, Fort Stockton 79735, 915/336-2264
Admission: $5 to water show

The water carnival starts Thursday night with a pageant followed by a musical production. Saturday features a parade and crowning of Miss Fort Stockton. The water show, which includes water ballet, takes place at an Olympic-size swimming pool at Comanche Springs. These springs used to spill forth 60,000 gallons of water a day until they ran dry in 1950 after years of irrigation. Wells drilled to water cattle and crops depleted the underground water supply.

Farwell
Bordertown Days
Last weekend in July
Farwell Chamber of Commerce, Box 117, Farwell 79325, 806/481-3681
Admission: free

Farwell gets together with Texico, New Mexico across the state line for a little summer fun. Saturday is the big day for this festival, with a parade in the morning, then live music all afternoon and arts and crafts booths. There's a rodeo Thursday, Friday and Saturday nights.

★

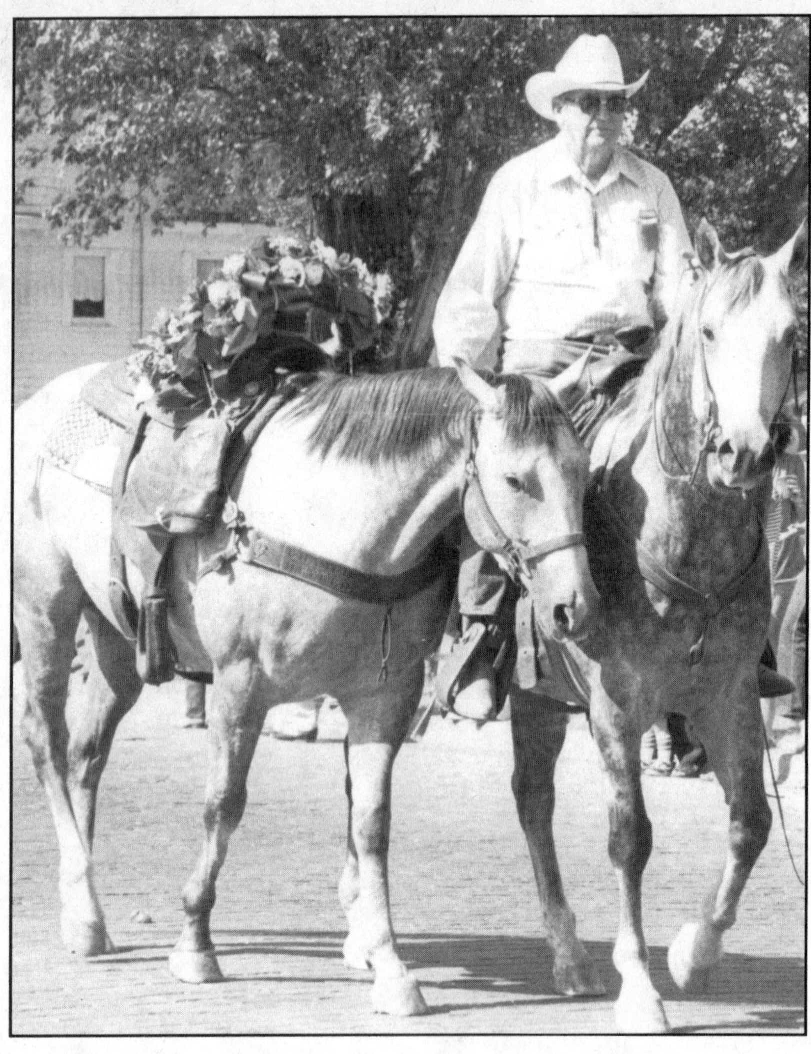

Finley Bradley leads the empty saddle horse at the head of the XIT parade in Dalhart. Photo courtesy *Dalhart Texan.*

AUGUST

Dalhart
XIT Rodeo and Reunion
First full weekend in August
Dalhart Area Chamber of Commerce, P.O. Box 967, Dalhart 79022, 806/249-5646
Admission to rodeo and dances

The XIT Ranch in the Panhandle, the largest ever inside one fence, once covered parts of 10 counties and 3 million acres. Since 1936, the festival has honored all who have worked on the ranch.

As many as 20,000 people attend each year to see the parade and rodeo, and to eat free barbecue and watermelon. There's a queen's contest, antique car show and the 5K Empty Saddle Run. The empty saddle theme, repeated in the parade and in a monument in Dalhart, pays homage to former cowboys who are now dead.

The XIT Ranch came into being when Texas needed a new capitol building in 1881. The state government had plenty of public land, but not much cash, so they paid contractors Charles and John Farwell 3 million West Texas acres to construct the capitol building.

Pecos
Cantaloupe Festival
First weekend in August
Pecos Chamber of Commerce, P.O. Box 27, Pecos 79772, 915/445-2406
Admission: $2

To celebrate the world-famous Pecos cantaloupes, this festival includes a dance, contests, arts and crafts, stage show, food booths and Little Miss Cantaloupe Pageant. Games include cantaloupe eating, rolling, seed-spitting, and look-alike contests. In the look-alike contest, participants shape the meat of a cantaloupe to look like their own faces.

Sunday features a fly-in at the airport. Airplane pilots compete at bombing targets with cantaloupes. There's also a breakfast at the fly-in with cantaloupe as a main ingredient.

Hereford
Town and Country Jubilee
Second week and weekend in August

Deaf Smith County Chamber of Commerce, P.O. Box 192, Hereford 79045, 806/364-3333
Admission to All-Girl Rodeo: $4

This celebration of life on the High Plains offers visitors the chance to see Hereford's famous All-Girl Rodeo, which runs Friday through Sunday nights. While you're in town, you can visit the National Cowgirl Hall of Fame, which pays tribute to women in ranching and rodeo, as well as those who had a hand in shaping the West.

The Jubilee includes two or three days of arts and crafts on display, a fajita cook-off, a 10K run, 2-mile run, fun walk, and wheelchair races. There's also a farmer's market, road rally, and concert by local musicians. Saturday is the main attraction with a parade, food, games, music all day in the park, and a dance.

Dimmitt
Harvest Days
Third weekend in August
Dimmit Chamber of Commerce, 115 W. Bedford, Dimmit 79027, 806/647-2524
Admission: free

This started as an old settler's reunion in the late 1950s, and is now combined with the Castro County Fair. Festivities include a parade, street dance, square dance, quilt show, comical style show, follies, volleyball tournament, chili cook-off, and a barbecue supper.

Sonora
Sutton County Days
Fourth weekend in August
Sonora Chamber of Commerce, P.O. Box 1172, Sonora 76950, 915/387-2880
Admission to rodeo and dance

Sutton County Days includes a parade, outdoor dances, a rodeo, a barbecue, a queen contest, arts and crafts, an old-time fiddler's contest, food booths, and a variety of other entertainment.

While you're there, you should visit the Caverns of Sonora, known as one of the world's most beautiful caves.

Pecos
Pecos River "Yacht" Race
Last weekend in August

Pecos Chamber of Commerce, P.O. Box 27, Pecos 79772, 915/445-2406
Admission: free to spectators

Pecos is an Indian word meaning "crooked," and during this annual river race, boaters find themselves heading north on a southbound river more than once. The event includes a 16-mile canoe and kayak race, as well as a six-mile "home-made" raft race just for fun.

Perryton
Wheatheart of the Nation Celebration
Last week in August
Perryton-Ochiltree Chamber of Commerce, P.O. Box 789, Perryton 79070, 806/435-6575
Admission: free except for dances and demolition derby

In 1947, Ochiltree County farmers raised more wheat than anyone else in the United States, earning their home the name "Wheatheart of the Nation." Still a leading wheat producer, the county remembers this honor with an annual celebration.

The second Saturday is the big day, beginning with a free breakfast. Other events include a parade, free barbecue meal, tractor pulls, demolition derby, 10K run, fun run, and two dances. The Museum of the Plains has an open house on Saturday, during which pioneer skills are demonstrated.

Fritch
Howdy Neighbor Day
Third Saturday in August
Fritch Chamber of Commerce, P.O. Box 396, Fritch 79036, 806/857-2458
Admission: free

The folks in Fritch have been saying howdy to their neighbors since 1959 with this festival. Activities include a parade, arts and crafts fair, stage show and food booths.

Nearby Lake Meredith offers a variety of recreation. The Alibates Flint Quarries National Monument has ruins of an Indian village from the days when Native Americans mined flint at the site.

Eldorado
Schleicher County Days and Rodeo
Second weekend in August
Schleicher County Chamber of Commerce, P.O. Box 1155, Eldorado 76936, 915/853-3109

Admission to some events

This festival features a parade, dance, rodeo, arts and crafts fair, live entertainment, and food booths. Games include dominoes, 42, washer and horseshoe pitching, an egg toss, and a tug of war.

SEPTEMBER

Balmorhea
Oasis of West Texas Festival
Labor Day Weekend
Balmorhea Chamber of Commerce, P.O. Box 272, Balmorhea 79718, call city hall at 915/375-2307
Admission: free

Held in downtown Balmorhea, this festival includes an arts and crafts fair, games, the World Championship Frijole Bean Cook-off, 10K and 2-mile runs, a horseshoe pitching contest, a bicycle parade, tortilla toss, egg toss, legs contest, food booths and plenty of live entertainment. The festival attracts about 1,000 people.

Friona
Maize Days
First or second week of September
Friona Chamber of Commerce and Agriculture, P.O. Box 905, Friona 79035, 806/247-3491
Admission: free

Most Maize Days activities take place on Saturday, including the parade, foot race, barbecue lunch, arts and crafts, food booths and street dance. Weekday activities include the carnival, a nighttime golf tournament with 9 p.m. tee off, and a night of family entertainment.

Maize Days originally celebrated the maize harvest. Now, although only a little maize is grown, they still have the festival, but it's earlier in the fall.

Harper
Frontier Days and Rodeo
Saturday and Sunday of Labor Day weekend
Harper Chamber of Commerce, P.O. Box 308, Harper 78631, 512/864-5656
Admission: $5 for rodeo, $4 for meal, $4 for dance

A parade gets festivities rolling in Harper Saturday afternoon. Other activities include two nights of rodeo, each followed by a dance, barbecue meals each evening, food booths, a rodeo queen contest, and a fiddler's contest on Sunday.

Marfa
Marfa Lights Festival
Labor Day weekend
Marfa Chamber of Commerce, P.O. Box 635, Marfa 79843, 915/729-4942

Reports of the mysterious Marfa Lights, often seen from Highway 90, nine miles east of the town, date back to the 1840s.

Some viewers compare the lights to car headlights, only larger, different colors, and higher in the air. They're often described as being far away over a flat area, sometimes in groups of three or four, sometimes single. The lights have been spotted from many vantage points in the area, both by people looking for them, and by unsuspecting travelers.

This may be the only festival in Texas with a round-table discussion as one of its events. Usually a few Marfa Lights experts are recruited to talk about sightings of the lights, theories of their occurrence and whatever else comes up. In 1989, panelists included a representative from the McDonald Observatory and Judith Brueske, Ph.D., author of a book about the lights.

In her book, *The Marfa Lights*, Breuske says theories for the existence of the lights abound. Explanations range from ghost stories to the possibility of St. Elmo's Fire, ball lightning, gases, glowing minerals, mirages, piezoelectricity, and even UFOs.

Besides the round-table discussion, the town puts together a parade, two dances, country music concerts, a Texas art show, an arts and crafts fair, food booths, games, chuckwagon breakfasts, and two nights of rodeo.

A time exposure of the Marfa Lights shows their movement against the background of the Chinati Mountains. Photo courtesy of *Big Bend Quarterly*.

Miles
Cotton Festival
Second weekend in September
Miles Preservation Authority, P.O. Box 367, Miles 76861, 915/468-3001
Admission: free except for dance

This festival raises money for the restoration and upkeep of the historic Miles Opera House, built in 1904 and listed in the National Register of Historic Places in 1976. The Opera House serves not only as an entertainment place, but also a meeting hall and senior citizen center.

Activities include a Saturday morning parade, an arts and crafts fair, a fun run, live music all day, a brisket cook-off, food booths, children's games, a horseshoe toss, an egg toss, washer pitching, and a street dance at night.

A country meal and barbecue supper are served in the opera house. Many events take place in the city park.

Stratford
Stratford Fair and Jamboree
Weekend following Labor Day
Stratford Chamber of Commerce, P.O. Box 570, Stratford 79084, 806/396-2260
Admission: free

Since 1945, Stratford has enjoyed this community gathering, which now includes a parade, a dance, crowning of the Old Timers King and Queen, a rodeo playday, and a chili cook-off. There's also entertainment in the park, a barbecue meal, a dog show, and tellers of tall tales. Exhibits include canning, horticulture, antiques, and china.

Quanah
Fall Festival
Second weekend in September
Quanah Chamber of Commerce, P.O. Box 158, Quanah 79252, 817/663-2222
Admission: free

This North Texas town, named after Comanche Chief Quanah Parker, marks the coming of cool weather with games, a street dance and food booths. There's a horseshoe pitching tournament, a car show, an arts and crafts fair, live music all day, children's games, a nail driving contest, and an ice melting contest.

Nearby Copper Breaks State Park offers camping areas and

the Quanah Parker Interpretive Center. The Center tells the story of Quanah Parker, as well as farming and ranching in the area.

Chief Quanah was the son of Cynthia Ann Parker, a white girl captured at age 9 by the Comanches in 1836. She eventually became a wife of Chief Nocona and gave birth to three children, including Quanah. By the time she was found by white settlers 20 years later, she thought of herself as an Indian. The return to white civilization took her from her family and way of life. She missed her tribe and the open plains that were her home, and died of sorrow only a few years later.

Her son Quanah grew up to be a strong leader, who resisted white settlers' advances until 1875, when he realized if his people were to live, they would have to accept the ways of "civilization." So Parker and his group settled on an Indian reservation.

Stamford
Stamford Country Fair/Stenholm Fun Day
First or second week of September and all day Saturday
Stamford Chamber of Commerce, P.O. Box 1206, Stamford 79553, 915/773-2411
Admission: free to fair; fee for Fun Day

Most of this festival takes place at Stamford's downtown Post Office Square. Events include a parade, dance at the rodeo grounds, classic car show, contests, arts and crafts, live music, food booths and hobby exhibits.

Lamesa
Fiesta
Third weekend in September
Lamesa Area Chamber of Commerce, P.O. Drawer J, Lamesa 79331, 806/872-2181
Admission: free

Hosted by the Mexican-American Community, this festival celebrates Mexico's Independence from Spain. Activities begin in the late afternoon each day and include a parade, a dance each night, contests, a stage show, food booths, and a volleyball tournament. You'll also find folk dancers, a low rider contest, piñatas, and live music.

Junction
Kimble Kounty Kow Kick
Labor Day
Kimble County Chamber of Commerce, 402 Main, Junction 76849, 915/446-3190
Admission: free

The Kow Kick features an old-time fiddler's contest, children's games, live entertainment, food booths and an arts and crafts fair. Games include horseshoe and washer tournaments. Quilts, photography and crafts competitions also take place.

Ballinger
Texas State Championship Pinto Bean Cook-off
Last weekend in September
Ballinger Chamber of Commerce, P.O. Box 577, Ballinger 76821, 915/365-2333
Admission: free

Besides the pinto bean cook-off, there's also a dance, games, arts and crafts fair and meal of beans and cornbread.

OCTOBER

Post
C.W. Post Founder's Day Celebration
Second weekend in October
Post Main Street Project, 105 E. Main, Post 79356, 806/495-4157
Admission: free except for rodeo, chuckwagon lunch, and ball

Post hosts an outdoor breakfast of cereal and orange juice at the world's longest breakfast table, which spans the length of the courthouse and seats 400 people. In honor of C.W. Post, the cereal magnate who founded the town, they serve Post cereal. Breakfast eaters get a nice view of hot air balloons taking off nearby.

Other events include a parade, dance, bicycle races, trail ride, Western art show, ranch hand competition, rodeo, live music and live theatre production. You can see hot air balloons, gliders, and arts and crafts, as well as partake of goodies from the food booths.

Snyder
White Buffalo Days Celebration
Second Saturday in October
Snyder Chamber of Commerce, P.O. Drawer CC, Snyder 79549, 915/573-3558
Admission: $1

This festival gets its name from the rare albino buffalo reportedly killed near Snyder by hunter J. Wright Mooar in the late 1800s. Activities include a parade, contests, arts and crafts, food booths and a melodrama play.

Canadian
Fall Foliage Festival
Third weekend in October
Canadian-Hemphill County Chamber of Commerce, P.O. Box 365, Canadian 79014, 806/323-6234
Admission: free; fee for homes tour

You'd think that out on the West Texas plains a tree would be about as common as a cactus in Wisconsin. Well, trees are the exception to the rule in the Panhandle, so maybe that's why the folks up there get so much pleasure from the trees that grow along the Canadian River. This big waterway gives life to some lush plant life near its shores, much of which turns bright red and gold in the fall. Some of the most colorful plants are the cottonwood tree, soapberry tree and sumac bush.

The Foliage Festival began in 1950 to satisfy a great interest in the fall colors. A trail ride offers a peaceful outing among the trees. If you don't have time for a wagon ride, you can drive your car (or bicycle) 10 miles along Formby Road from Canadian to Lake Marvin to take in the scenery. There's also an arts and crafts fair, live entertainment, food booths, tour of homes and a car show.

Brownfield
Harvest Festival
Third Saturday in October
Brownfield Chamber of Commerce, P.O. Box 152, Brownfield 79316, 806/637-2564
Admission: free

This festival celebrates the cotton, wheat and sorghum harvests, and gives everyone in Brownfield a chance to get out and have a good time. They have a parade, an old-time fiddler's contest, live entertainment all day, the crowning of the Harvest Queen, prize drawings, and food booths.

Del Rio
Fiesta Amistad
Weekend nearest October 24
Del Rio Chamber of Commerce, 1915 Ave. F, Del Rio 78840, 512/775-3551
Admission: free

Fiesta Amistad features the only parade in the world that starts in one country and ends in another. The 10K run and bicycle races both start in Del Rio and end across the border in Ciudad Acuña.

Fiesta Amistad, which means friendship festival, commemorates the date of the first summit meeting between presidents of the United States and Mexico. In 1960, Eisenhower met with Adolfo Lopez Mateos on United Nations Day.

Other activities include a two-day arts and crafts fair, food booths, and a battle of the bands in which groups from both cities compete for prizes. You'll also find a Miss Del Rio Pageant, a fajita cook-off, and the Laughlin Air Force Base open house and airshow.

Top photo: Men hurry toward the finish line in the pumpkin rolling contest in Floydada's Punkin Days. Photo courtesy *Floyd County Hesperian.*

Bottom photo: Costume contest winners show off their duds during Floydada Punkin Days. Photo courtesy *Floyd County Hesperian.*

Floydada
Punkin Days
Last weekend in October
Floydada Chamber of Commerce, P.O. Box 147, Floydada 79235, 806/983-3434
Admission: free

Pumpkins are a major crop in Floyd County, which is known as "Pumpkin Capital, U.S.A." The festival features pumpkin rolling races, a pumpkin pie contest, pumpkin painting and pumpkin carving. The wheelbarrow race challenges blindfolded drivers to follow directions of passengers loaded down with pumpkins to the finish line.

Alice Gilroy, publisher of the *Floyd County Hesperian*, said she enjoys the pumpkin painting. "We have a lot of artistic people in town who paint the pumpkins. It's just beautiful."

The festival, she said, focuses on participation, and everyone gets involved and has fun. "The only complaint we've had is that it's over too soon."

Other activities include a parade, a masquerade dance, an arts and crafts fair, and food booths. Most events take place Friday and Saturday nights.

November

Terlingua
World Championship Chili Cook-off
First Saturday in November
Sam Lewis, 420 N. Van Buren, San Angelo 79601, 915/658-1432
Admission: $10 for two days

This world-famous event helped establish chili as an important dish in American cuisine. Begun in 1967, this is the original cook-off, after which all others are modeled.

It started as a competition between Wick Fowler, that renowned Texas chili cook, and a restaurant owner in California to see if Texas or California chili was best. Now the event attracts about 10,000 spectators each year.

Visitors enjoy the antics of the chili cooks, many of whom enter the showmanship competition as well as cooking. Cooks must compete in other cook-offs all over Texas and the U.S. for enough points before they may enter the contest at Terlingua.

Folk musician Gary P. Nunn plays Friday and Saturday night each year. You'll find plenty of beer, various games and thousands of chili-loving party-goers just hanging around waiting for a taste.

Terlingua has no motels, but Study Butte, just a few miles down the road, has three. Lajitas on the Rio Grande, a resort, is about 24 miles away. You need to call months ahead if you want to stay at one of these places. But Sam Lewis, who helped found the cook-off and who still maintains the festival site, said the best thing to do is bring your tent, camper or R.V. and camp on the grounds. The atmosphere is friendly and there's plenty of room, he explained.

★

DECEMBER

Del Rio
Lake Amistad Festival of Lights Parade
Second Saturday in December
Del Rio Chamber of Commerce, 1915 Ave. F, Del Rio 78840, 512/775-3551
Admission: free

A nighttime lighted parade of boats decorated in the spirit of Christmas floats by several vantage points for visitors to Lake Amistad.

The parade passes westerly along the south shore of the San Pedro Campground and Black Brush Point park sites, then along the cliffs of Diablo East Park to Governor's Landing at the Herb C. Petry Bridge. From there, the boats return to Diablo East Marina, where they are judged.

Cities

Austin

Fiesta Laguna Gloria
Third weekend in May
P.O. Box 5568, Austin 78763, 512/458-8191
Admission: $5

More than 200 artists from all over the United States show their work in the largest juried exhibit of its kind in the nation. Strolling through the beautifully landscaped museum grounds, you'll find ethnic foods, music and children's activities, as well as some great art.

Juneteenth
June 19
Austin Juneteenth Committee, 2912 E. 14th Street, Austin 78702; call Rosewood Park at 512/472-6838 or Novella Cabin at Givens Recreation Center, 512/928-1982
Admission: free

Rosewood Park is the site of this Emancipation Day celebration, where visitors will find music, food, children's activities, sports tournaments, fireworks and a black history program. It all starts with a parade that morning.

Aquafest
Last weekend in July and first two weekends in August
Aquafest, 811 Barton Springs Road, Austin 78704, 512/472-5664
Admission: fees range from free to $8

A land parade, water parade and a multitude of water activities at Town Lake make Austin Aquafest one of the most popular festivals in the state, showcasing Austin's musical talent and recreational opportunities.

A total of 90 bands perform on four stages during the festival, offering visitors a smorgasbord of music. There are also dance shows, game booths, arts and crafts booths, a bike race and bike tour, police rodeo, plays, and food for sale.

Corpus Christi

Czech Heritage Festival
Early March
Czech Heritage Society of South Texas, P.O. Box 1974, Corpus Christi 78403-1974, 512/882-9226
Admission: $5

Held in the Bayfront Plaza Exhbit Hall, this event offers a generous portion of Czech culture, with music, food and exhibits. You'll see folk dance, music and gymnastic performances during the day. In the evening, a traditional Grand March of Czech costumes precedes several hours of dancing to some of Texas' best Czech polka bands.

You'll also find Czech foods, arts and crafts and cultural exhibits. In the afternoon, you can tour the historic Jalufka House in Corpus Christi's Heritage Park. This home, built by James Jalufka in 1908, has been refurbished by the Czech Heritage Society and now houses a Czech geneological and photo library. The building is surrounded by rose gardens designed to match the original gardens planted by Jalufka.

Buccaneer Days
10 days in late April
Buccaneer Days Commission, P.O. Box 30404, Corpus Christi 78404, 512/882-3242; for accommodations info call Convention and Visitors Bureau at 512/882-5603
Admission: free; fees for some events

Corpus Christi celebrates the discovery in 1519 of Corpus Christi Bay with parades, music, a sailboat regatta, water sports events, fireworks and a carnival. Contestants in the Buccaneer Days pageant act as pirates who force the mayor to walk the plank off a boat into the waters of the bay.

Bayfest
Last weekend in September or first weekend in October
Bayfest, P.O. Box 1858, Corpus Christi 78403, 512/887-0868
Admission:free

A special event during this festival is the spirited tugboat competition, wherein professional tug captains push barges through an obstacle course. Other attractions include a boat parade, art fair, fireworks, five stages featuring continuous

Corpus Christi Mayor Betty Turner gets the traditional mayor's dunking during Buccaneer Days.

entertainment, games, food booths, and a cultural and educational area. For kids, there's a tent where they can try their hands at various crafts and games, as well as carnival rides. Visitors can buy a ticket to the Texas State Aquarium and ride a water taxi from the festival grounds to the aquarium and back.

Dallas

Artfest
Memorial Day weekend
8300 Douglas, Suite 800, Dallas 75225, 214/361-2011
Admission: yes

Fine arts and crafts attract thousands of visitors to this pleasant festival at Fair Park. There's music, food and several large tents where artists show their work.

State Fair of Texas
Two weeks in October
State Fair of Texas, P.O. Box 26010, Dallas 75226, 214/565-9931
Admission: $7 adult; $4 kids and seniors

Three million people visit the nation's largest state fair every year. You'll find exhibits, midway rides, food, music , fireworks and other entertainment.

El Paso

Fiesta of the Arts
Three days ending with July 4
Chamizal National Memorial, Superintendent Franklin G. Smith, 700 E. San Antonio, Room D301, El Paso 79901, 915/534-6277
Admission: free

Music, dance and art from both sides of the border highlight this festival held at the Chamizal National Memorial.

Border Folk Festival
First weekend in October
Chamizal National Memorial, Superintendent Franklin G.

Smith, 700 E. San Antonio, Room D301, El Paso 79901, 915/534-6277
Admission: free

Dancing, folk music, arts and crafts and outdoor stages await visitors at the 55-acre memorial grounds.

Galveston

Mardis Gras
Two weeks in February, ending Sunday before Ash Wednesday
Galveston Convention and Visitors Bureau, 2106 Seawall Blvd., Galveston 77550, 409/763-4311
Admission: free; fee for some events

This traditional pre-Lenten festival features colorful parades, balls, pageants, costume contests and art exhibits. The Grand Night Parade takes place the Saturday before Ash Wednesday, even in freezing weather. Galveston's Mardi Gras attracts as many as 200,000 visitors.

Dickens on the Strand
First full weekend in December
Events Department, Galveston Historical Foundation, 2016 Strand, Galveston 77550, 409/765-7834; in Houston, 713/280-3907
Admission: $6 adult; $3 kids over 6 and senior citizens; free for those wearing Victorian costume

Galveston's Strand, named after the Strand street in London, was the heart of Texas commerce in the late 1800s until a hurricane destroyed the city in 1900. Now, each December, the street becomes a replica of the Strand in London to usher in the Christmas season. Visitors will find street entertainers, strolling carolers, parades and characters from Charles Dickens' novels roaming about. Vendors sell food such as plum pudding, roast pig, roasted chestnuts and other English fare. The Dickens Handbell Festival, the largest handbell performance in the world, takes place Saturday evening. Visitors will find hand made Christmas items for sale.

Houston

Houston Livestock Show and Rodeo
Mid-February through early March
Houston Livestock Show and rodeo, P.O. Box 20070, Houston 77225, 713/791-9000
Admission: $5 adult general admission to rodeo; reserved seats higher

Centered around the largest stock show in the nation, events include rodeo, nightly musical entertainment, a trail ride and various contests. It all takes place at the Astrodome.

Houston International Festival
Two weekends in March or April
Houston International Festival, 1221 Lamar, Houston 77010, 713/654-8808
Admission: free

The International Festival usually focuses on a particular country each year. One year it was Japan, another Australia. You'll find outdoor entertainment downtown around Jones Hall, Tranquility Park and Sam Houston Park, including dancing, music, art, crafts and food.

Greek Festival
First full weekend in October, Thursday, Friday and Saturday
Greek Orthodox Cathedral, 3511 Yoakum Blvd., Houston 77006, 713/526-5377
Admission: $2 evenings and Saturday

What may be the oldest ethnic festival in Houston offers about 30,000 visitors a look at Greek culture. Activities include dancing, dance performances, music, Greek travel films and church tours. You'll find Greek food galore, an icon display, a Greek market and a gift shop.

San Antonio

Riverbottom Festival and Mud Parade
One weekend in January
Paseo del Rio Association, 213 Broadway, Suite 5, San Antonio 78205, 512/227-4262
Admission: free

Each January when the Riverwalk canal is drained for maintenance and repairs, folks get together for a procession along its banks, highlighted by the Mud King and Queen. Attractions include mud games, music and dancing.

Carnaval del Rio
Five days before Ash Wednesday
Paseo del Rio Association, 213 Broadway, Suite 5, San Antonio 78205, 512/227-4262
Admission: free

This Mardis Gras festival features a different ethnic theme each night, such as Cajun, Mexican or French. Visitors will find music, food, and floating bands. A children's area with storytellers, clowns, animals and musicians makes this a family event.

Fiesta
Week during which April 21 falls
San Antonio Visitor Information Center, 317 Alamo Plaza, San Antonio 78205, 800-447-3372
Admission: varies for different events

Fiesta is a giant salute to the Texian Army's victory over Mexico's General Santa Anna at San Jacinto in 1836. This battle on April 21 effectively freed Texas from Mexico, enabling it to become an independent nation.

This week-long citywide festival has something for everybody, all over town. Three parades entertain visitors — a river parade, a daytime street parade, and a nighttime parade. You can see arts and crafts galore, hear plenty of good music, and enjoy dancing and food.

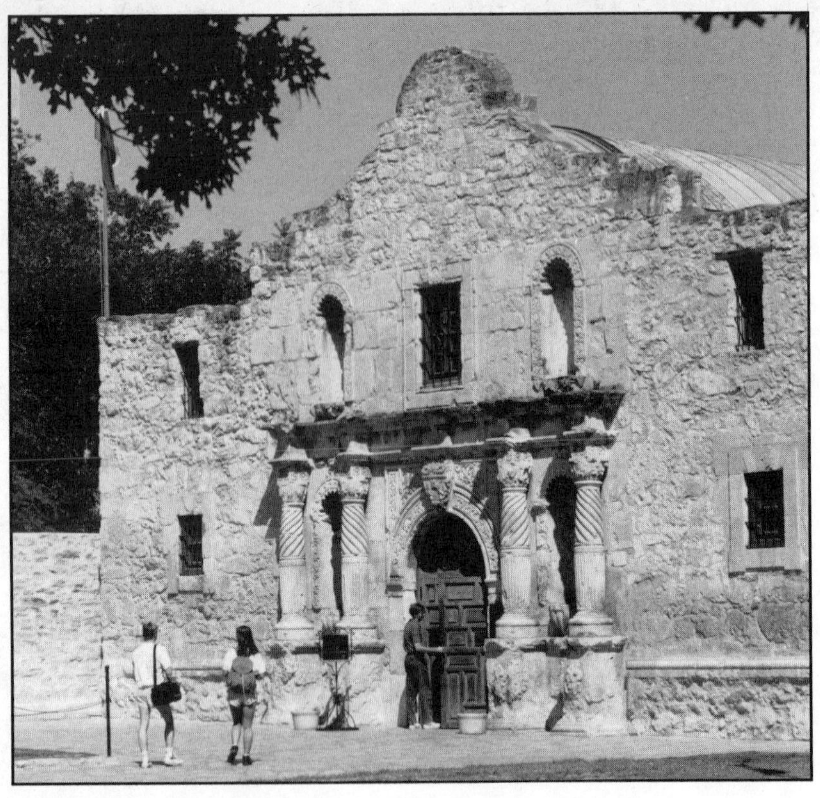

The Alamo is a year-round attraction in San Antonio.

Cinco de Mayo
Weekend nearest May 5
Jessie Moreno, Market Square, 514 West Commerce, San Antonio 78207, 512/299-8600
Admission: free

Celebrating the Battle of Puebla, this event offers food, music, a parade and all kinds of live entertainment. Market Square is San Antonio's Mexican-style marketplace.

Texas Folklife Festival
First weekend in August
For festival information: The Institute of Texan Cultures, P.O. Box 1226, San Antonio 78294, 512/226-7651
For hotel, motel and RV park info: San Antonio Convention and Visitors Bureau, P.O. Box 2277, San Antonio 78298, 1-800-447-3372
Admission: $6 adult, $2 kids 6 to 12

One of the biggest events in the state, this annual celebration of our ethnic and cultural diversity attracts over 120,000 people. It takes place on the Institute of Texan Culture's 15-acre festival grounds in Hemisphere Plaza in downtown San Antonio.

More than 30 ethnic groups serve food, demonstrate crafts and perform music and dancing. You'll see people dressed in all kinds of costumes, from pioneer garb to Indian ceremonial feathers. You'll see quilters, spinners and weavers.

You can taste Lebanese meat loaf, Greek Spanokopita, Dutch ice cream, Scottish shortbread and Vietnamese fried banana. You can also get roasted peanuts, pickled pig's feet, yam pie and strawberry wine. And of course, chicken fried steak, chili, tacos and barbecue.

You can get advance purchase discounts on tickets. It's not easy to park near the festival grounds, so each year they arrange easy-to-use park and ride bus service. Call or write to find out about parking.

Diez y Seis
Weekend closest to Sept. 16
Jessie Moreno, Market Square, 514 West Commerce, San Antonio, 78207, 512/299-8600
Admission:free

This event celebrating Mexican Independence Day offers food, music, and a fun atmosphere. Most events are held at Market Square, the city's Mexican market.

Great Country River Festival
Late September
Paseo del Rio Association, 213 Broadway, Suite 5, San Antonio 78205, 512/227-4262
Admission: free

This country and western music festival features bands playing at the outdoor Arneson River Theater, as well as other locations along the riverwalk, including in boats.

Index

A

B

C

G

H

N

T

U

V

W

X

Y

Texas Festivals makes a great gift for friends or relatives. To order more books, just fill out the following order form and mail it to us.

ORDER FORM

Quantity	Price each	Total
	$9.95	
Texas residents add 7.75% sales tax (.77 per book)		
$2 for shipping and handling		2.00
Total enclosed		

Send books to:

Name

Address

City State Zip

Make check or money order payable to Palmetto Press and mail to:

Texas Festivals
619 Betty Street
El Campo, TX 77437